How Do I Get to Know God?

Books in the Life-Transforming Truths from a Never-Changing God Series

Other Books by D. James Kennedy

How Do I Get to Know God?

Life-Transforming Truths from a Never-Changing God

Book 2

D. James Kennedy

Fleming H. Revell
A Division of Baker Book House Co
Grand Rapids, Michigan 49516

Published by Fleming H. Revell
a division of Baker Book House Company
P.O. Box 6287, Grand Rapids, MI 49516-6287

Printed in the United States of America

Library of Congress Cataloging-in-Publication Data

Kennedy, D. James (Dennis James), 1930–
    Life-transforming truths from a never-changing God / D. James Kennedy.
       p.   cm.
    ISBN 0-8007-5558-8 (bk. 1)
    ISBN 0-8007-5557-X (bk. 2)
    ISBN 0-8007-5559-6 (bk. 3)
    Contents: bk. 1. What is God like? — bk. 2. How do I get to know God? — bk. 3. How do I live for God?
    1. Theology, Doctrinal—Popular works. 2. Christian life. 3. Westminster Confession of Faith. 4. Fundamentalist churches—Doctrines. I. Title.
[BT77.K2767   1995]
  230′.044—dc20   94-179918

Contents

Introduction

It was first uttered on a night illumined by a singular star.

A whisper issued from a manger.

It had about it the lisp of baby speech, yet the ears of wise men tuned to hear across a pain-wracked world.

Behold a promise:

"I am he who makes all things new."

That word was heard again on a night of earnest questions.

Now a Teacher breathed the words.

"Nicodemus, except a man be born again, from above, he shall in no wise enter the kingdom of heaven."

"But how . . . "

"I am he who makes all things new."

The words came again, this time with a dolorous tone.

Night fell at noonday without a star.

The Son of God hung outside the wall, as the very triunity of God was ripped apart. God become man became sin.

"*Tetelestai*"—"It is finished."

"Now all things can become new."

The word burst, fire-tongued, on a morning that needed no star.

A grave stood gaping.

Death was swallowed; life returned to a shrouded
    world that still listens for a final trumpeted victory
    salute.

The song will resound:

"I am he who makes all things new."

These words glide gently through the gloom to a
    twilight soul.

Suddenly it's morning.

Though corrupt in flesh, an inner man awakens young
    and fresh—everything backwards from what we'd
    expect.

"Begin again," he calls,

He who makes all things new.

*H*e will make you new. That promise is
repeated over and over in Scripture. It
is both the promise of God and the
experience of history.

The first of our three books on the transforming doctrines or teachings of Scripture presented a travelogue
of the quest toward a higher understanding of ourselves, our world, and the God who is. We ended that
book at the brink of a high, dark precipice, where the
creature crafted to glorify and enjoy God forever
plunged from God's sight. If we can nudge our quest
metaphor just a little further, we now stand still and
watch God's own quest unfold—the quest of the plan
of salvation in Jesus Christ. Only Christ can speak the
words with which we begin: "I am he who makes all
things new."

For reasons we have already made clear, only one set
of truths can unravel the story of this second quest. We

can look with confidence only to the Bible, God's sufficient and utterly trustworthy revelation of himself. Again we will also take advantage of one of the most systematic outlines ever written to describe what the Bible teaches. This most helpful outline is called the *Westminster Confession of Faith* and its companion *Larger* and *Shorter* catechisms. Like any creed or confession that Christians have written and used over the years, the Westminster standards are only aids to understanding Scripture. Written in the 1640s, some of the involved sentences in the Westminster standards may seem a lot of trouble to sift through. Yet the trouble is repaid, for the insights of these men of God are the fruits of deep thought, fervent devotion, and earnest prayer. Are there any three things our society needs more than these?

I have three readers in mind in offering this book. First, I warmly desire to share the basics of Christian faith with anyone who does not know the Christ of Scripture and of the cross. For this reason I have made every effort to answer questions that non-Christians have asked me over the years and to be clear about what we believe and why. Second, I hope this book and its two sister publications will enable and encourage Christians to share their Lord and Savior with others. Third, in an era in which the Christian church so often speaks with a wavering tongue and a mouth full of mush, may these words call you to deeper, clearer, faith—with love and without compromise. One caveat must be understood: We will approach the transforming themes of salvation. They have utterly changed my life, and they continue to renew my heart at each encounter. Yes, you can reject the Christ of Calvary and go your way, but you will never be the same as if you had never met and heard him speak. You can decide to remain nominally identified with "religion," deciding that wholehearted discipleship and turning from your lifestyle just isn't for you. But you will be forced to make a decision, and it may not be as easy to remain neutral as you think. These themes of Scripture are transformers. One way or the other, you will be changed when you encounter the real Jesus of Nazareth.

Consider, for example, Jacob DeShazer, a crack bomber pilot at the start of World War II. DeShazer joined the elite unit of volunteers who flew with Jimmy Doolittle on that first bombing raid on Tokyo. Only DeShazer was shot down on that historic raid. Captured, and incarcerated in a Japanese prison, he was tortured regularly. As a result DeShazer developed an intense hatred of everything Japanese. He survived with only one thought: to get his hands on the throats of his tormentors.

One day there came into his possession a copy of the New Testament. He opened it and heard its mysterious proclamation: "Behold, I make all things new." As he came to understand and believe the gospel, Jacob DeShazer was made new. The hatred drained away, and his heart was filled with love. He returned to Japan as a missionary after the war and wrote his story in a pamphlet distributed around Japan.

Mitsuo Fuchida also was a pilot at the beginning of World War II. In fact, Captain Fuchida led the air assault on Pearl Harbor, giving the final "All squadrons attack!" order that sent 360 planes loaded with death down upon the ships. When the day was over, the planes had killed more American sailors than had died in all of World War I, and Fuchida was the national hero of Japan. Yet in the end came defeat and disillusionment. He dreamed of a world without war, but it seemed impossible. *Peace*, *brotherhood*, and *love* were meaningless words.

Then one day in a train station Fuchida picked up one of DeShazer's tracts. Here was a man whose heart had been changed by a power Fuchida could not imagine. He read the gospel presentation and right then was transformed by the power of Christ. Fuchida too became a missionary, a preacher to his own people. In the city where both Buddhism and Shintoism had first entered Japan, the commander of the raid on Pearl Harbor spoke to a gathering of 2000 Japanese about the God who can change hearts, no matter who you are.

No matter who

Has your life been transformed? Two kinds of people have trouble accepting the message of transformation. One is the person who feels he or she is "good enough" and in no need of change to be acceptable before God. The other is the person who believes he or she is too bad, that Christ "would never want me." When I think of that second category I recall a man who was about as worthless and derelict a person as I ever heard of. Some decades ago this man was an alcoholic who spent most of his time looking for ways to get a bottle on the streets of Chicago. Whatever little money he could make from the jobs he could keep for a few days was spent on whiskey.

Unfortunately, this man had a wife and daughter. He neglected them, deprived them of food, even beat them during his drunken rampages. One day his precious little blonde daughter became ill. Her mother had hidden a little emergency cash, so there was money to buy medicine. Only the father took this money and went out and bought booze. By the time he sobered up his little girl was dead. He went in to see his daughter laid out dead in her tiny, simple coffin. As he looked down at her through his tears he took off her shoes. He sold them and got drunk again.

This time when he half sobered he figured that he was too bad to exist in the world. Slowly and painfully he began the trek across town to Lake Michigan, intending to throw himself in the lake. On the way he passed a rescue mission where somebody was preaching. A loudspeaker on the street blared out the words of grace about One who could give a new heart, a new character, a new life. As the words flowed over him like fresh water the man was cleansed. His heart was transformed, and he became a new man mightily used by God. Eventually he established one of the most successful missions this country has ever seen. It still is being used to reach and change worthless people.

It is astounding how many are willing to trade the outer trappings of religion for the inner reality that possesses that power. They devour the husk and discard the kernel. As a result, our churches, our lives, our families, and our society are dying from spiritual malnourishment. Many drunks and drug addicts have passed into eternity without a Savior, when the reality was right there, waiting to free and transform them. So have religious people who relied on something other than the reality of a new and changed heart.

Five words that transform lives

In the ministry of Evangelism Explosion we have a simple, effective way to share how Jesus Christ changes lives. As we begin a study of salvation, I want to introduce five words that are easy to remember and stand at the center of all else that will be said here. These words are:

1. Grace
2. Man

3. God
4. Christ
5. Faith

1. Grace

    a. Heaven is a free gift
    b. It is not earned or deserved

This is the starting point for understanding and sharing the gospel. And what a startling idea it is. Most people think heaven is something you earn by being good. But it is not. Heaven is a gift that is decidedly not earned or deserved: "For by grace are ye saved through faith; and that not of yourselves: it is the gift of God: Not of works, lest any man should boast" (Ephesians 2:8–9).

2. Man

    a. Is a sinner
    b. Cannot save himself

That seems pretty clear, especially to anyone who has come to understand that each human being stands guilty of breaking God's law. People are sinners and nothing they do could ever make them good enough to earn a place in heaven: "For all have sinned, and come short of the glory of God" (Romans 3:23). The importance of this comes through when you see what Scripture says about God.

3. God

    a.   God is merciful
    b.   God is just

God wants us to be with him in heaven. He wants us to have eternal life—to be all that we were created to be eternally. But he also is just. He must judge our sins or he will not be a God worthy of the name. They have to be paid for if his justice is to be satisfied. Though he says, "I have loved thee with an everlasting love" (Jeremiah 31:3b), "Thou art of purer eyes than to behold evil, and canst not look on iniquity" (Habakkuk 1:13a). He does not leave the guilty unpunished (Exodus 34:7).

Here is where Christ comes in.

4. Christ

   a. Who he is: The infinite-eternal God-man
   b. What he did: Died on a cross to purchase a place for us in heaven

God's love is clearly seen in Jesus. He became human, though he is the eternal God. And he died on a cross though he was sinless. He died to pay for our sins. In this he shows God's love and fulfils God's justice. He died so we do not have to. "The Word was made flesh, and dwelt among us" (John 1:14). "He [God] hath made him to be sin for us, who knew no sin; that we might be made the righteousness of God in him" (2 Corinthians 5:21). He became sin so that we might be forgiven.

Now that he has risen from the dead he offers eternal life to anyone who will receive it by faith.

5. Faith

   a. What it is not: intellectual assent or temporal faith
   b. What it is: trusting in Jesus Christ alone

Faith is the key to heaven, but it is not just knowing about Jesus Christ. Nor is it trusting God for such things as safety, health, and wealth, which are temporal and will pass away. Saving faith is trusting in Jesus Christ alone for our salvation. Only as we depend totally on him can we know that God has forgiven us and made us new. "Believe on the Lord Jesus Christ, and thou shalt be saved" (Acts 16:31).

This is the gospel: It is that easy and that impossible. Through such good news Christ transformed Saul of Tarsus on Saul's way to persecute Christians. Through such good news Christ transformed a hateful Jacob DeShazer and a hopeless Mitsuo Fuchida. Through such good news Christ transformed a wretched derelict on his way to die. In our own way each of us who have life in Christ were once wretched derelicts on our way to die.

That is what makes these transforming truths such good news.

How did Jesus Christ make a way to God?

It pleased God, in his eternal purpose, to choose and ordain the Lord Jesus, his only-begotten Son, to be the Mediator between God and man, the Prophet, Priest, and King; the Head and Saviour of his Church, the Heir of all things, and Judge of the world; unto whom he did, from all eternity, give a people to be his seed, and to be by him in time redeemed, called, justified, sanctified, and glorified. [Westminster Confession of Faith, chapter 8]

1

All Things Are Made New

The Bible addresses itself to all sorts of questions: Questions that are theological and moral. Questions that are ethical and intellectual. Questions that are spiritual and physical. Questions that are existential and eternal.

We sought answers for some of the most basic of these in book 1, finding the only ultimate answer in God. The answers to the "quest questions"—Who am I? What is my purpose in living? Why is the world as it is? Is anyone in control of life?—transform our lives as they unveil the Creator in whom we live and move and have our being. Knowing God lifts human beings from futility to significance.

Yet some of the answers point us to the bad news of humanity's lost condition. It is not enough to know the answers if we cannot use them to transform our ethical, intellectual, spiritual, physical, existential, and eternal selves. The bottom line is this: *Men and women must be made new.* The old analogy of the caterpillar becoming the butterfly has been overused. So have Jesus' words: "Except a man be *born again*, he cannot see the kingdom of God" (John 3:3b). Yet these two pictures vividly tell the story of the gospel, and the reason why that story is so unpopular in our time.

Caterpillars do not live very exciting lives. They never travel far, they must expend much effort to journey what little distance they do move, and when they reach their destination what do they see? More dirt. One day two caterpillars were making their way across a particularly muddy terrain when a butterfly fluttered by. One of the caterpillars stopped to watch as the butterfly dipped and flitted, carried here and there in the wind currents. He turned to his companion in the mud. "You'd never get me up in one of those things!"

What is in a name?

Lots of people feel the same way about being reborn in Christ. Back in the 1970s Watergate scandal conspirator Chuck Colson described his own spiritual journey to Christ in the book entitled *Born Again*. Suddenly everyone in the media and politics was talking about "born-again Christians." A man sitting next to me on a plane at that time asked if these "born-again people" were starting some kind of new religious sect.

> *Therefore if any man be in Christ, he is a new creature: old things are passed away; behold, all things are become new. And all things are of God, who hath reconciled us to himself by Jesus Christ.* [2 Corinthians 5:17–18a]

"No," I said, "they've been around quite a while. In fact, the only kind of Christian that exists is a born-again Christian, whether he be Presbyterian, Methodist, Roman Catholic, Greek Orthodox, Lutheran, or whatever. Unless a Christian has been born again, that person is not a Christian in anything other than a merely nominal sense of the word."

It is a small wonder those looking at the church from the outside become confused. What a plethora of types of "Christians" and sorts of allegedly Christian behaviors abound! Protestants kill Catholics in Northern Ireland and vice versa. Modernists, Barthians, and inerrantists fight over the sense in which the Bible is God's Word. Colleges that have traditions steeped in faith teach evolution and sponsor homosexual student associations.

At the turn of the century a group of American businessmen and theologians published a series of twelve books called *The Fundamentals* to explain that not all Christians deserve the term. Out of those popular books was born a new category of Christian—*Fundamentalist*. If Muslim fundamentalists blow up airliners and assassinate, what might Christian "fundies," as they are sometimes called, be up to? Some were dissatisfied with the fundamentalist label and founded a new movement to set out the essential differences between true Christianity and the modernist. This movement chose an old Reformation word, *evangelical*, to describe a faith that was Bible-centered, Christ-focused, and evangelism-minded. But before long some began to co-opt the evangelical banner for a wide variety of very bad theological positions. Now we euphemistically call the evangelical churches that have slipped toward heresy "broadly evangelical." They are evangelicals, sort of.

Similar confusion attached to those who have focused on sanctification and the work of the Holy Spirit, while retaining allegiance to the fundamental teachings of Scripture. The names *Pentecostal* or *Holiness* have described such churches, though a variety of teachings, some of them patently unbiblical, have occasionally skewed that focus. *Charismatic renewal* movements have sought to return mainline churches to a purer Christianity from within, but such reformations face the danger of going off in unscriptural tangents. Pentecostal and charismatic fellowships range from the most vibrant centers for worship, discipleship, and witness to anemic, emotion-driven encounter groups with some connection to the "charismatic" gifts of speaking in tongues, prophecy, and healing.

Many other labels have invaded the church of Jesus Christ and hit the secular newsstands. Some labels identify cults whose doctrines have only the most superficial connection to Christianity. Labels grow from legitimate differences of opinion among brothers and sisters who share allegiance to Christ as Savior and Lord and Scripture as the unerring revelation of God to us. Too frequently, however, the labels mask attempts to replace historic faith with something more "relevant" and friendly to the anti-Christian world. My companion on the jetliner had every right to be confused.

Oh, to sweep away the labels. Let the humanists, modernists, and any other "ists" find their own religious names; calling oneself a rocket scientist won't get anyone a step closer to the stars and calling oneself "Christian" or "born again" won't get one a whit closer to God.

A Christian is a life transformed—remade into something new—by God in Jesus Christ.

The life cycle of rebirth

The life cycle stages of a butterfly are egg, larva, pupa, adult. Each signals a basic change in lifestyle and being. But only the metamorphosis from caterpillar to butterfly deserves to be called a rebirth. Likewise, there are passages in the life cycle of a human being, each traumatic and being-altering in its own right—womb to infancy; toddlerhood to childhood; adolescence to young adulthood; middle to old ages. Only one metamorphosis is rebirth, however, when a person passes from the living death of the state of sin to the state of eternally living life in a new covenant of grace between human being and God.

The new covenant of grace actually is an ancient agreement. When all things were new, God established another agreement, which sometimes is called a "covenant of life," with Adam, the first human being. Adam was on the spot in this covenant; he was responsible to obey its one command. This was a covenant of life in which Adam and his descendants could live forever, enjoying God and glorifying him, if Adam did not cross the line into disobedient rebellion. When he did cross that line the covenant of life was shattered, but God was ready with another covenant that provided a way back from sin and death (Genesis 3:16–17). This way back was a plan for new birth, newness that could only come through payment of the eternal penalty for sin.

This new covenant could have only a new kind of Mediator, One who was both God and man. From the very moment when he was born of a virgin, until he was laid in a new tomb, Jesus constantly made things new. He took what was old, dying, and dead, and changed them. Now ruling in heaven he continues to make things new, and will until that climactic day when he says, "I make all things new" (Revelation 21:5b). Then he will create a new heavens and a new earth (Revelation 21:1).

Imagine following Jesus around on a day of his earthly ministry, especially during those last months when his work was building to a climax. Had we been there, following a mile or so behind the rabbi from Nazareth, we might have encountered a man and two women who are talking and gesturing excitedly with their friends.

"Sir, I seek the teacher," we interrupt.

"Ah, you want to see Jesus," the man replies with a nod.

"Yes, you must meet him. I have come to love him more than life itself, and he has given me life of more than one kind. My name is Lazarus. A week ago at about this time, I died."

"You mean you became sick enough to die."

"I mean just that I *died*! My body was empty, and it was wrapped with spices and laid in a cave until my flesh would rot away. Then Jesus came by. I was made alive."

Considering this strange story, we proceed down the road until we come to the tax booth of Zacchaeus. We have heard about this agent of Rome who is particularly hated because of the unfair fees he charges. But now the fee is quite reasonable, lower than that of any other tax collector.

"Oh, pay what you can afford," he says with a laugh. "I *was* a cheat and a thief, if the truth be known. But then Jesus passed by. When everyone else hated me, he singled me out from the crowd to love, and now my life is new."

We meet a lame man who runs and jumps. We encounter one who had been a stinking leper, but who now hurries from person to person to show that his skin is fresh and pure, like that of a baby. A once-blind beggar embraces us with the exciting news that Jesus of Nazareth has come by and heard his cry for mercy. He marvels for the first time at the colors of the surrounding hills and sky.

Children and adults, young and old. The Master has left a wake of change. All things and all people are changed, one way or the other, when they encounter Jesus. Some are hardened to hate him; others are forever softened by renewed body, mind, and spirit.

To understand the dynamics of rebirth we must understand two people. First we must meet Jesus, the One in whom a person can become reborn. Second, we must get to know the changed person who has met Jesus along the way.

One who changes things

When an informed Old Testament believer took a dove or a lamb to the temple at Jerusalem the worshiper understood that this sacrificed animal's death would not take away sin. In those times when Scripture was taught, prophets and priests clearly explained that sacrifices were a shadow—a token of love and obedience by the worshiper, and a token of the true removal of sins that would occur when *Messiah* came.

Messiah. The very word told something about this future person, for the word means "the anointed one." The messiah would be miraculously empowered by God, anointed and ordained for the great task. There was much Old Testament people did not know about this coming Savior, but those who studied the prophets could have explained that the Anointed One would be a Prophet, a Priest, and a King:

A Prophet

A prophet is one who speaks for God among the people. Old Testament prophets were directly inspired by God and spoke out from a direct communication. Much of the writing of the Old Testament, such books as Isaiah, Jeremiah, Hosea, Amos, and Malachi, record these inspired prophetic communications. Prophets were middle-men, mediating God's Word to his people. The Anointed One would be the once-and-forever Prophet:

> The LORD thy God will raise up unto thee a Prophet from the midst of thee, of thy brethren, like unto me; unto him ye shall hearken. . . . I will raise them up a Prophet from among their brethren, like unto thee, and will put my words in his mouth; and he shall speak unto them all that I shall command him." [Deuteronomy 18:15, 18–19; see Matthew 21:11; Luke 24:19; John 4:19; Acts 3:22; Acts 7:37]

> The spirit of the Lord GOD is upon me; because the LORD hath anointed me to preach good tidings unto the meek; he hath sent me to bind up the broken-hearted, to proclaim liberty to the captives, and the opening of the prison to them that are bound. [Isaiah 61:1; see Matthew 11:5; Mark 1:14; Luke 4:14–21; Luke 8:1]

The *Westminster Shorter Catechism* describes Christ's prophetic work this way: "Christ executeth the office of a prophet in revealing to us, by his word and Spirit, the will of God for our salvation."

A Priest

Protestants tend not to talk of priests. We do not have such mediators—but that is not true at all. We have a priest. The point where we differ is that we believe no *other* priest is needed. For our Priest also is the King. Genesis 14 introduces a king who was a priest, a mysterious character named Melchizedek. Abraham encountered him at Salem, the mountaintop Canaanite village where, centuries later, the city of Jerusalem would stand. We know only two things about Melchizedek. First, he ruled the peoples who had settled this land. Second, he represented the people in worship before God.

A priest became a vitally important person centuries later when the nation of Israel received God's laws. The primary function of priests was to slaughter the animals brought by the people as sacrifices for sin. Priests burned those sacrifices on the altar as offerings to God. They also prayed for the people and participated in celebrations of worship. Once each year, on the Day of Atonement, the high priest entered the Holy of Holies, the room set apart to symbolize God's holiness, containing the ark of the covenant that symbolized his presence. For one moment each year this mediator offered full intercession for the people, asking that God's wrath for their disobedience might be turned away. But the nation awaited the coming of an ultimate priest who would be the final mediator of the law and the one who would offer the final cleansing sacrifice for sin:

> The LORD hath sworn, and will not repent, Thou art a priest for ever, after the order of Melchizedek. [Psalm 110:4; see Hebrews 5:5–10; 6:19–20; 7:15–25]

> Therefore will I divide him a portion with the great, and he shall divide the spoil with the strong; because he hath poured out his soul unto death: and he was numbered with the transgressors; and he bare the sin of many, and made intercession for the transgressors. [Isaiah 53:12; see Hebrews 7:26–28; 9:11–14, 24]

Behold the man whose name is The BRANCH; and he
shall grow up out of his place, and he shall build the
temple of the LORD: Even he shall build the temple of
the LORD; and he shall bear the glory, and shall sit and
rule upon his throne; and he shall be a priest upon his
throne: and the counsel of peace shall be between them
both. [Zechariah 6:12b–13; see Hebrews 9:24; 1 John
2:1]

The *Westminster Shorter Catechism* describes
Christ's priestly work in the offering up of himself as
a sacrifice to satisfy divine justice, his reconciling people to God, and his continual intercession before God
for us.

A King

Even without the example of Melchizedek, Old Testament people knew that the Messiah would end the
need for a king or any other ruler. His heritage would
be of the royal family of David, and his dynasty would
never end. Some things only a few Old Testament
prophets understood. Surely Isaiah had the clearest
picture of it. The new kingdom would be no earthly
empire, but rather a spiritual realm. It, therefore, could
cross national and ethnic boundaries. It was a rule of
the heart. Also, the reign of the King himself, and not
just a king's family, would be eternal.

Did Jesus fulfil all of this prophecy? After all, the
line of kings was established through the father, and
we say that Jesus was the Son of God, not of Joseph.
The early readers of Matthew's and Luke's genealogies
were not bothered by this in the least. There was no
distinction between sons by blood and sons by adoption in that culture. The declaration of sonship was the
deciding factor, not genetic relatedness. Joseph read-

ily adopted Jesus into the Davidic family. This custom prepared the people, not only for Jesus' unique sonship, but for ours in him—adoption as the children of a heavenly Father. The following are just a few of the prophecies that the Anointed One would be the final Mediator of the kingdom and family of God:

> Yet have I set my king upon my holy hill of Zion. [Psalm 2:6]

> The days come, saith the LORD, that I will raise unto David a righteous Branch, and a King shall reign and prosper, and shall execute judgment and justice in the earth. In his days Judah shall be saved, and Israel shall dwell safely: and this is his name whereby he shall be called, THE LORD OUR RIGHTEOUSNESS. [Jeremiah 23:5; see John 1:49; 18:33–37]

> David my servant shall be king over them; and they all shall have one shepherd: they shall also walk in my judgments, and observe my statutes, and do them. And they shall dwell in the land that I have given unto Jacob my servant, wherein your fathers have dwelt; and they shall dwell therein, even they, and their children, and their children's children for ever: and my servant David shall be their prince for ever. [Ezekiel 37:24; see Matthew 2:5–6; Luke 1:32–33]

The *Shorter Catechism* says that "Christ executeth the office of a king, in subduing us to himself, in ruling and defending us, and in restraining and conquering all his and our enemies."

The Head and Savior of his church

Other religions have had messiahs of a sort. Confucius was a great teacher, Mohammed a self-styled prophet who became much like a king to the nomadic peoples of his time. But as a Prophet, a Priest, and a King, Jesus uniquely came to save a people for God. His was a "search and rescue mission." Moreover, he did not found an empire but an international refuge, gathering from among every people those he had rescued. This is something the likes of which the world has never seen except in the church, a society of worshipers without ethnic, nationalistic, class, cultural, or racial barriers, whose charter was signed in blood and whose by-laws were founded on love for others before self. The church hasn't always lived like that, but the church truly headed by Jesus Christ is supposed to be that kind of nation.

This unique relationship often allowed those early prophets to see their coming Anointed One as mediator of a new kind of nation:

> Also the sons of the stranger, that join themselves to the LORD, to serve him, and to love the name of the LORD, to be his servants, every one that keepeth the sabbath from polluting it, and taketh hold of my covenant; Even them will I bring to my holy mountain, and make them joyful in my house of prayer: their burnt offerings and their sacrifices shall be acceptable upon mine altar; for mine house shall be called an house of prayer for all people. [Isaiah 56:6–7; see Romans 10:12–13]

> And it shall come to pass, that whosoever shall call on the name of the LORD shall be delivered: for in mount Zion and in Jerusalem shall be deliverance, as the LORD hath said, and in the remnant whom the LORD shall call. [Joel 2:32; see John 4:21–24]

> For he hath looked down from the height of his sanctuary; from heaven did the LORD behold the earth . . . to declare the name of the LORD in Zion, and his praise in Jerusalem; When the people are gathered together,

and the kingdoms, to serve the LORD. [Psalm 102:19, 21–22; see Acts 15:12–18]

In chapter 25 of the *Westminster Confession*, the headship of Christ over the church is described: "The visible Church, which is also catholic or universal under the gospel (not confined to one nation as before under the law) consists of all those, throughout the world, that profess the true religion. . . . Unto this catholic visible Church Christ hath given the ministry, oracles, and ordinances of God, for the gathering and perfecting of the saints, in this life, to the end of the world; and doth by his own presence and Spirit, according to his promise, make them effectual thereunto."

Heir to and Judge of the world

The irony of describing Christ as Heir is that he is the Creator, and all things have been his from the beginning. Still, in the plan of grace Christ gave up what was his by right and assumed the subordinate role of servant. Even those looking forward to the coming of their Anointed One, however, knew that the role of servant would fall away in the day of accounting, revealing a Messiah who was also Judge.

Christ, then, is the Mediator of justice. He truly defines what justice is, and the day of his coming is a day of uncovering truth and dispensing judgment:

He shall not judge after the sight of his eyes, neither reprove after the hearing of his ears: But with righteousness shall he judge the poor, and reprove with equity for the meek of the earth: and he shall smite the earth with the rod of his mouth, and with the breath of his lips shall he slay the wicked. And righteousness

shall be the girdle of his loins, and faithfulness the girdle of his reins. [Isaiah 11:3b–5]

Behold, the LORD hath proclaimed unto the end of the
world, Say ye to the daughter of Zion, Behold, thy salvation cometh; behold his reward is with him, and his
work before him. [Isaiah 62:11; see Luke 2:11; John
4:42; 1 John 4:14]

Chapter 33 of the *Confession* points to the final day
of justice, administered by Jesus, the anointed Judge:
"God hath appointed a day wherein he will judge the
world in righteousness by Jesus Christ, to whom all
power and judgment is given by the Father."

These and many other prophecies tell the ways that
Jesus Christ mediates the covenant of grace and the plan
of God. The most important of these to remember are
the first three. Jesus Christ is Mediator of the covenant
of grace as a Prophet, as a Priest, and as a King. All other
ways can be thought of as fitting under one of those
headings, but all are important to our understanding of
the Messiah and the changes he brings.

The question for all time

If that is the shape of the Christ who makes people new,
what is the shape of a new person? We can see the
difference when the pupa cocoon of a caterpillar discloses
its changed inhabitant. Reborn people are not quite so
obvious. What is new about the newborn child of God?
A man named Nicodemus was a teacher of the law, yet
he did not understand the answer to that question. As
told in John 3, he sought Jesus out at night, whether
secretly out of fear to be associated with this new teacher
or because he wanted uninterrupted time in which to be

taught. But Jesus immediately understood Nicodemus's lack of awareness and answered the question that Nicodemus and every other person in history had feared to ask:

"No one can see the kingdom of God unless he is born again."

Jesus laid it on the line. He was saying something much like this:

"Nicodemus, here is the teaching you are missing, and it is not optional. If you are not made new, you are outside the kingdom of God; you are blind to spiritual reality; you cannot understand spiritual truths, and you shall never enter the kingdom of God."

What imperious words, yet they stand eternally true. Unfortunately, the ways people try to become new show no more understanding than did Nicodemus.

"What do you mean, Lord? Do I have to go back into the womb again?"

"No, Nicodemus. You must be born from above. Only the Holy Spirit makes you new."

Had we been standing there, listening in, we might have jumped in at this point.

"What do you mean, Lord? Will not my good works suffice?"

"If you had any piety (and you have none) it would not make you new. Only perfect righteousness is good enough. Come to me and believe."

"What do you mean, Lord? Surely my baptism and church membership punch my ticket?"

"I alone am the way, the truth, and the life. No other ticket exists. Come to me and believe."

"What do you mean, Lord? Surely if I follow the 'golden rule' and live by the Ten Commandments you won't turn me away?"

"If you come before me on that basis you will not see God. Only trusting in me makes all things new."

"You must be born again." What a sweeping condemnation of all that we are, all that we have, and all that we have done. We need an entirely new life, a new heart, a new soul. True religion begins on the inside. But again the Nicodemus in us asks: "How does one know?" In response, Jesus took Nicodemus back to one of the first stories he had probably learned as a child (Numbers 21). During their years of wandering in the wilderness the children of Israel had rebelled against God (as usual), and in judgment he had sent venomous snakes through the camp. Only Moses had the antidote: God instructed Moses to make an image of a snake wrapped around a staff. Those who looked on that cross-like form did not die from the venom. Now Jesus reminds Nicodemus of how those snake-bitten Israelites had passed from death to rebirth:

> As Moses lifted up the serpent in the wilderness, even so must the Son of man be lifted up: that whosoever believeth in him should not perish, but have eternal life. . . . And this is the condemnation, that light is come into the world, and men loved darkness rather than light, because their deeds were evil. For every one that doeth evil hateth the light, neither cometh to the light, lest his deeds should be reproved. But he that doeth truth cometh to the light, that his deeds may be made manifest, that they are wrought in God. [John 3:14–15, 19–21]

We are so familiar with John 3:16 that we may overlook its main point. God so loved that he gave his only Son in Jesus that whosoever looks on the cross in the same way those sinful, dying Israelites looked on that other cross will live. That is the way to become new. The Israelites were in the darkness of rebellion. They were dying from God's judgment for that rebellion. They had to:

1. *Realize* their true condition. Realization meant confession that the serpents were sent from God, who had afflicted them for good cause.
2. *Believe* the promise.
3. *Obey.* Literally lift venom-clouded eyes from the darkness to the light of that gleaming cross.

Paul says that the secret to becoming a new creation is to be "in Christ. . . . old things are passed away; behold, all things are become new" (2 Corinthians 5:17). Paul tells us the same thing Jesus told Nicodemus. To be reborn three crucial things are necessary.

1. The sinner must *realize* that he is a sinner, dead to God and bound for damnation through the venomous serpent's bite of rebellion against the God of the universe.
2. The sinner must *believe* the gospel: that God sent his one and only Son, who became sin and paid the penalty, crucifying the serpent of sin in his own body on the cross; that Jesus arose victorious over death and the grave on the third day.
3. *Obey.* The sinner must look on that cross as his own, accepting Jesus as Savior and Lord, stepping from darkness into the light so that everyone can see what has happened in the sinner's life.

Are you a creature made new? If so, has your life stepped into the light so that the world can see that most dazzling of miracles—not the caterpillar turned gossamer butterfly but the rebel turned reconciled child of God?

How can someone come to Christ?

All those whom God hath predestined unto life, and those only, he is pleased, in his appointed and accepted time, effectually to call, by his Word and Spirit, out of that state of sin and death, in which they are by nature, to grace and salvation by Jesus Christ; enlightening their minds, spiritually and savingly, to understand the things of God; taking away their heart of stone, and giving unto them a heart of flesh; renewing their wills, and by his almighty power determining them to that which is good, and effectually drawing them to Jesus Christ; yet so as they come most freely, being made willing by his grace. [Westminster Confession of Faith, chapter 10]

2

The Hound of Heaven

Francis Thompson's vivid metaphorical poem, "The Hound of Heaven," portrays a great chase. A fugitive seeks to escape a relentless hunter. The pursuer is always coming, never hurrying yet never breaking off nor slowing. He does not see but he knows, for he hears the footsteps and the voice—the voice reminding him that flight is futile.

I fled Him down the nights and down the days;
   I fled Him, down the arches of the years;
I fled Him, down the labyrinthine ways
   Of my own mind; and in the midst of tears
I hid from Him, and under running laughter,
     Up vistaed hopes, I sped;
     And shot, precipitated,
Adown Titanic glooms of chasmed fears,
   From those strong Feet that followed, followed after.
     But with unhurrying chase,
     And unperturbèd pace,
Deliberate speed, majestic instancy,
     They beat—and a Voice beat
     More instant than the Feet—
"All things betray thee, who betrayest Me."

Here and there he runs, always coming eventually to a dead end. Finally cornered, the vanquished waits, seeing at last the approaching conqueror:

Naked I wait Thy love's uplifted stroke!
My harness piece by piece Thou hast hewn from me,
    And smitten me to my knee;
    I am defenceless utterly.
    I slept, methinks, and woke. . . .
I stand amid the dust
    o' the mounded
    years—
My mangled youth
    lies dead beneath
    the heap.
My days have crack-
    led and gone up in
    smoke,
Have puffed and
    burst as sun-starts
    on a stream.

Book 1 proclaimed that God is sovereign Ruler of the universe. He does not work helter-skelter, nor does he ad-lib as he goes along day by day. Rather, he laid the architectural plans for all his work before he created the world. He sovereignly controls and ordains that which shall come to pass, managing the greatest star and the least atom.

> *Lo, every one that thirsteth, come ye to the waters, and he that hath no money; come ye, buy, and eat; yea, come, buy wine and milk without money and without price. . . . Incline your ear, and come unto me: hear, and your soul shall live.*
> [Isaiah 55:1, 3a]

Yet this governance leaves a certain natural liberty to people. Adam and Eve were created and given a covenant of life by God. They stood with a choice before them: They could submit to God and his wonderful plan for their lives, glorifying God, administering his creation, and enjoying his fellowship forever. Or they could cross the line into disobedience by breaking the one negative command God had given, expressing rebellion that desired to usurp God's prerogatives and authority. The choice was ultimately between life and death. The freedom of all the human race rested on the shoulders of its first member.

"I fled him"

The choice, of course, was made, plunging humanity with all creation into a chaotic bondage and condemnation. Knowing all things, the Creator had already planned for the consequences of this rebellion. The covenant of life lay in pieces, but he raised a greater covenant in its place, a promise of grace that rested in a new Adam, one provided personally by God. By this grace a call goes out to all God's enemies. A life of blind hopelessness—a starvation of the soul—afflicts those who have not trusted in Christ for redemption. A life of futility and an eternity of hell await.

Yet the voice of God calls: "Come to the waters, all who are thirsty. You who have no money, come and eat! All of you, Hear me and live." Some seem to hear only a faint echo off distant mountains; some hear the footsteps distinctly but successfully evade the persistence of the call, until its sound finally fades to silence. And for some, the hound of heaven persists, on and on and on and on—never hurried but never stopping, until the restless soul is invaded by love.

"All things betrayest thee"

We should not say more than does the Bible about God's call to the soul, but we also must say as much, so we can better understand salvation in Jesus Christ. Scripture tells us of two calls:

The external call

There is an external call to every human being on planet earth. God's plaintive invitation reaches out in love to all humanity. It is that free invitation of the gospel that we share universally (see, for example, Matthew 28:19–20 and John 3:16). Accompanying this invitation is the command to repent and turn from sin to Christ or face destruction (for example, 2 Chronicles 30:8; Jeremiah 4:4; Nahum 1:2–3; Romans 2:5–8).

> *Moreover whom he did predestinate, them he also called: and whom he called, them he also justified: and whom he justified, them he also glorified.*
> [Romans 8:30]

The internal call

There is an internal call that the heart hears and answers. God's call through the Holy Spirit enlivens the dead hearts of those he has chosen from all eternity to save. Scripture refers to these as the *elect*. Those from every tongue, kindred, nation, and tribe who hear this call answer, because they know God sent his Son to die and to procure eternal life for them.

This question of how God calls is answered through the doctrine of predestination, a subject that divides Christians, who interpret the passages on predestination with some variation. If you trust in Christ as the Son of God, born of the virgin, crucified on the cross in your place, resurrected and seated at the right hand of God the Father, your Savior and Lord, then I will not withhold fellowship from you as a brother or sister in Christ because we disagree about what the Bible teaches regarding election and predestination. I hope you feel the same toward me. At the same time, I am writing about tenets that transform faith and churches as we better understand and apply them. I place God's predestinating love and his "hound of heaven" call among the transforming articles of faith.

The Bible speaks of a call that is effectual and a call that does not lead to new birth. When I say in the name of Jesus Christ, "Ho, every one that thirsteth, come ye to the waters, and he that hath no money; come ye, buy, and eat; yea, come, buy wine and milk without money and without price. . . . Incline your ear, and come unto me: hear, and your soul shall live," I address non-Christians who do not feel the slightest spiritual thirst. Their soul-throats are parched and dry, but they do not see their need. Their emotions are hardened and their eyes blinded because that is the natural state of each fallen man and woman. Therefore, something more than an external invitation must happen. There must be an inward work of the Spirit of God, effectually drawing the individual and opening his or her eyes to see the real situation. Only then is the person able to be willing to choose Christ freely.

That the *outward* call of the gospel is of limited effect may be seen in Matthew 22:14: "For many are called, but few are chosen." That "few" still contains a multitude no one can number. That the *inward* call of the Spirit is effective can be seen in John 6:37: "All that the Father giveth me shall come to me; and him that cometh to me I will in no wise cast out" and Romans 8:30: "Moreover whom he did predestinate, them he also called: and whom he called, them he also justified; and whom he justified: them he also glorified."

Those God called came, even though they did not deserve to hear that call because of any good in themselves. Those God did not call did not come, but they did not deserve to hear it either:

> Reprobate silver shall men call them, because the LORD hath rejected them. [Jeremiah 6:30]

> What then? Israel hath not obtained that which he seeketh for; but the election hath obtained it, and the rest were blinded (According as it is written, God hath given them the spirit of slumber, eyes that they should not see, and ears that they should not hear:) unto this day. [Romans 11:7–8]

> For this cause God shall send them strong delusion, that they should believe a lie: That they all might be damned who believed not the truth, but had pleasure in unrighteousness. [2 Thessalonians 2:11–12]

"Thy love's uplifted stroke"

But what of the inward call, the one God works in the heart through the Holy Spirit? The *Westminster Confession of Faith* says at least six things about it:

First, grace irresistibly draws a person in God's time, not ours. A delightful Southern preacher named Kennedy Smartt has dedicated his life to evangelism and has introduced perhaps thousands to the Savior, but he has felt a particular burden for one of his friends. Unless that prayer has been answered before you read this, Kennedy still prays each day for his lost friend, anticipating God's saving work in this man's life.

This prayer for his friend has only been part of his daily routine for a little over sixty years.

Acts 2:39 suggests that we should look for God to work in us and our children and even those who are far off, perhaps both in geographical distance and in their distance from God. It is a bittersweet moment when a sinner who comes to the Lord wishes to share that moment with a believing mother who has gone to the Lord. The mother never saw her prayers answered. Yet they were answered.

Second, grace irresistibly draws as the Holy Spirit applies the content of God's Word. "So then faith cometh by hearing, and hearing by the word of God" (Romans 10:17). I remain skeptical of great, emotional conversion experiences that arise from a vision or emotional event, having little or no discernible connection with the reading or teaching of the content of Scripture. Experiences that are real come because the Holy Spirit uses what the individual knows of Scripture (2 Thessalonians 2:13). But I fear that many come not to Christ but to psychological catharsis.

Third, grace irresistibly draws the person away from a life and worldview. Early in Billy Graham's crusade ministry he achieved a great deal of publicity when the mobster Mickey Cohen came forward and confessed Christ. But Graham quickly saw that Cohen was making no noticeable move to distance himself from his criminal empire. Billy made an appointment to see Cohen and confronted him with Scripture's demand for holiness. The mobster was surprised. If Christians could continue in their life's occupations, why should he have to change his? He, like the rich young ruler confronted by Jesus, turned away. This does not mean the newly saved person has left behind all sin, but it does mean the time to begin turning has arrived. The old ways should become uncomfortably foreign and undesirable, for "it is God which worketh in you both to will and to do of his good pleasure" (Philippians 2:13).

Fourth, grace irresistibly draws the mind to desire to know and love God. The enlightened mind of which the *Confession* speaks has no room for a vacuum. As the new believer turns from the old ways and ideas, his heart hungers to replace those things with truth and wholeness, "that by his power he may fulfil every good purpose of yours and every act prompted by your faith" (2 Thessalonians 1:11b NIV). The most beautiful sign that a miracle has occurred is not that a person stops swearing or using drugs or gossiping or flying into a rage at the least provocation. The beautiful thing is when swearing *is replaced* by words of kindness, when using drugs or sex to escape is replaced by an energetic aliveness to God and healthy relationships with others, when rage and bitterness are replaced by patience and emotional maturity. Such healing takes time, and often help from counselors and loved ones. That it can happen is a miracle.

Fifth, grace irresistibly renews the heart. "Create in me a clean heart, O God; and renew a right spirit within me," pleaded a repentant David in Psalm 51:10. Paul saw such a change in the Thessalonian believers: "Knowing, brethren beloved, your election of God. For our gospel came not unto you in word only, but also in power, and in the Holy Ghost, and in much assurance" (1 Thessalonians 1:4–5a). This heart renewal is the pre-eminent miracle of salvation, for it begins the restoration of what was lost in the fall. The writers of the *Confession* saw this as (1) taking away the heart of stone and replacing it with a heart of flesh, (2) renewing the will so that it desires to *serve* God and not to *be* God, and (3) focusing the mind on a new set of ideals—those that are "good." This is where irresistible grace tears out my old principle for living and installs a new principle. At this point Jesus becomes not just Savior, but also Lord.

Sixth, grace irresistibly draws the saved sinner ever closer to fellowship with Jesus Christ. In 2 Corinthians 5:11–21 Paul describes this drawing to Jesus Christ as reconciliation. Paul speaks of Christ's love constraining him, compelling him into the world as a witness, for Paul's wants have died in the One who died for him. Once he had a fleshly view of Christ and the world, but now "If any man be in Christ, he is a new creature: old things are passed away; behold all things are become new. And all things are of God, who hath reconciled us to himself by Jesus Christ, and hath given to us the ministry of reconciliation" (vv. 17–18). God has reconciled Paul irresistibly and irrevocably to himself. That could happen because Paul is identified in Christ crucified. That fellowship in the cross now impels Paul back out into the world as Christ's ambassador, imploring others: "Be ye reconciled to God" (v. 20).

"I am defenseless utterly"

What an incredible story this is: Jesus Christ, the Hound of heaven, tracked my fleeing soul down the immense halls of the years. The Holy Spirit called me irresistibly into the banqueting hall of the Father to partake of an eternal repast set with my name on it before the world began. And he has set me apart to be his ambassador to call the world to share in this meal of life in Christ. He has given me a share in searching out those others he intends to call to his great feast. There are two immense implications to the Bible's teachings about predestination and election. First, I am utterly ennobled and empowered by what has been done on my behalf. Second, I am utterly cast down and my egocentric spirit broken by how little all of this has had to do with me. The Christian who truly considers his or her salvation must be nearly pulled apart by the conflicting themes of glory and worthlessness.

> For whom he did foreknow [set his love upon], he also did predestinate to be conformed to the image of his Son, that he might be the firstborn among many brethren. Moreover whom he did predestinate, them he also called: and whom he called, them he also justified: and whom he justified, them he also glorified. [Romans 8:29–30]

> I will say to them which were not my people, Thou art my people; and they shall say, Thou art my God. [Hosea 2:23b; see Romans 9:25]

Paul presents a progression of events that have taken place in the name of each elect person. God *foreknew* them. There are two meanings this Greek word translated "foreknew" could take, but it can have only one meaning in Romans 8:29. The meaning this word does *not* have is that God knew what was going to happen ahead of time, saw who was going to choose him, and elected them. "Foreknew" here means that God set his intimate affection on the people he predestined, called, justified, and glorified.

One reason I believe this is verse 28. Paul says that all things work together for good—but *only for those who love God.* That makes sense, but Paul isn't finished yet. He says these people who love God are those who have been called according to his purpose. So which comes first, our love or God's call? It would seem most definite that those who love are those who were called. Now add in verse 29, as Paul explains further what he means in verse 28. Who loves? Those who are called. Who are called? Those on whom God has set his affection. Does it really make sense that we love *because* we were called, and we were called *because* God saw that we would love?

Another reason is that through all of Romans 7 and 8 Paul is speaking of the powerlessness of the individual over the law of sin and death. The human being is part of a frustrated creation. Suffering and degradation is the lot of all things, until God sets them to rights. Paul has particularly said in 8:5–8 that the mind of the sinful human being is set on death. The natural human being is hostile to God. The human mind "is not subject to the law of God, neither indeed can be. So then they that are in the flesh cannot please God." So where does this love arise in the human mind?

Third, Paul seems to anticipate our natural inclination not to want to accept this, for the primary purpose of Romans 9 addresses this very matter. The bottom line answer is 9:16: "So then it is not of him that willeth, nor of him that runneth, but of God that sheweth mercy." As the old hymn put it:

> I sought the Lord, and afterward I knew
> He moved my soul to seek Him, seeking me;
> It was not I that found, O Saviour true,
> No, I was found of Thee.

Fourth, only a view that God chose those he had set his intimate love upon conforms with the rest of Scripture, for the Bible says that faith is a gift (John 6:44, 65; 1 Corinthians 4:7; Ephesians 2:8; Philippians 1:29). The idea of this divine affection is found in Genesis 18:19 and Jeremiah 1:5. In fact, it pervades Scripture.

Many—a majority of Christians, in fact—do not agree with this position. There are two schools of thought, or two theological systems within Protestantism, which attempt to answer the question of how we come to choose God. The system I believe Scripture teaches is called *Calvinism*, after the Reformer John Calvin. Actually he took the concepts (aside from his reading of Scripture) in earlier Christian thinkers, especially Augustine. Most Christians take the other view and are called *Arminians*, after the theologian Jacob Arminius, though he was also teaching the thoughts of others before him.

Why do some accept and some reject the gospel? The Calvinist believes the difference is to be found in *God*, while the Arminian finds the difference in the *person*. The Arminian believes that God certainly provides the way of salvation, but each person makes the final determination about the fate of his or her eternal soul. The old saying is: "God votes for us; Satan votes against us, and we cast the deciding vote." This is an interesting little ditty, which would sum up salvation handily if it were true. The Bible-believing Arminian believes that salvation is a gift—unearned, unmerited, undeserved. But at the same time he or she wants to keep the human free will autonomous to choose God. And if both of those statements are true, and the Bible's picture of the human fall also is true, then not a single person will choose God, and no one will be saved. "What good is a 'whosoever will' in a world where everybody won't?" asked Charles Spurgeon.

Spurgeon is making the crucial point: The Calvinist is not saying that a person is not free to do what he or she *wants* to do. Every person is always free to do what he or she *wants*. The person is not free—does not have the power because of sin—to do what he or she *ought*. The person who ought to love God with heart, strength, mind, and soul is shackled by sin, and only the power of God, working through the Spirit in the inner call to the heart, can hold down the rebellious prisoner and break off the shackles that have made all the *wants* the *ought nots*.

"Those strong Feet that followed"

This may seem a minor shading in the big picture of salvation, hardly one of the life-transforming concepts promised. Also, many Arminian brothers and sisters have been far more humble servants of the Father and more aggressive ambassadors for Christ in the last century than many Calvinists. The story is told that nineteenth-century revivalist Charles Finney was accosted by a woman who said, "Mr. Finney, I don't like the way you do evangelism." Finney is said to have replied dryly, "Madam, I like the way I do evangelism a lot better than the way you don't do it." Finney's theology was superficial and appealed to an emotional response in a manner that has haunted American evangelism ever since. Yet many, many people truly came to know the Lord through his ministry because he gave himself wholeheartedly to the gospel.

However, the effectual call of God cuts to the heart of where we stand in relation to ourselves, to God, and to the unbelieving world. There are reasons God has gone to great lengths through Scripture to make it known to us.

In relation to ourselves

It seems a great danger that Christians who believe in the autonomy of the human will should set themselves on a higher moral plane from the non-Christian. The Arminian system says God offers eternal life to everyone, and some will believe and accept it and others will not, only because of some personal openness or closed-heartedness to Christ within the heart. "I have heard the gospel; I believe and accept Christ, therefore, I have eternal life," thinks the Christian. "You, neighbor, have heard the same gospel but because of your sinful and hard heart you've turned your back and rejected it. Therefore, you are not saved and I am. You are a different sort than I. In fact, I am more spiritual, more religious, more softhearted, less in love with sin and the world. Therefore I will cling tenaciously to something in which I can boast. If I cannot boast of my good works, I shall at least boast of my faith."

A person who has come to believe in the effectual call of God on his or her life cannot make such a statement and be consistent. In the presence of the non-Christian the believer must think: "I am truly no different than you. I could never have freed myself from my sins, just as you cannot. Eternal life is only mine because of the strong Feet that followed as I fled the Hound of heaven. I was in bondage, and only the Son of God could set me free (John 8:36). I was an unclean thing and nothing clean could have come from me (Job 14:4)." Lazarus, whom Jesus raised from the dead, would have sounded pretty silly if he had shouted into the tomb where a deceased friend lay buried and said, "I was obviously a lot more alive than you are, Eleazer. I hopped out of my grave, and I wasn't even stinking."

A spiritual Lazarus who understands fully that the only thing that makes his call from the tomb different was the authority of the caller, is transformed in self-awareness. A proper understanding of the call of God to our carcasses should squelch our feelings of self-sufficiency and lay us in awed, worshipful silence. "But he that glorieth, let him glory in the Lord" (2 Corinthians 10:17). This is a transforming glorying in Christ.

In relation to God

If God offers to all the choice and it is up to each person to accept, the implication is that God is desperately scrambling around the earth to coax all he can into the kingdom. Again, there is a grave danger, perhaps unconsciously, for the Arminian to hear God saying, "It is my will that everybody in the world should be saved. But, alas, in the end I must say, 'Not my will but yours be done. For you, O man, are the sovereign lord of this world, not I.'"

Through just such a view of dependent God and autonomous humanity did the pollution of humanism pollute the church, poisoning its pure waters. This is especially true in the popular theology that came into the church through such evangelists as Finney, who held just such a view of God and people. Finney wrote a book, which is still widely read and lauded today, called *Revivals of Religion*. It was the premise of this book that the salvation of people is not a supernatural work. Finney believed that revivals and other works of evangelism simply use the means God has afforded us to convince others. Finney was trained as an attorney, and he saw the witness for Christ as arguing the case for Christ as in a courtroom. How persuasively the Christian presents the evidence and uses good psychology to work on the emotions and break down that autonomous will are the fundamental factors of revival. Finney specifically rejected the effectual call of Christ and made the Holy Spirit subservient to the wit and cunning of the witness who pleads Christ's case.

Yet Ephesians 1:9 and other Scriptures state unequivocally that God is absolutely sovereign over all things, including the spirit, will, and heart. Romans 9:19 says that none resist his will. Do we have a God who is desperately trying to save everybody and is, for the most part, failing? Or do we have a God who has set his purpose and fixed his intimate delight upon a remnant for himself, those chosen from the foundation of the earth and unfailingly brought in his time into glory? God could be equally just and merciful if he never saved anyone. Spurgeon said that the amazing thing is not that everybody is not saved, but that anybody is saved. God issues the call to all humanity, commanding, "I have no pleasure in the death of the wicked; but that the wicked turn from his way and live: turn ye, turn ye from your evil ways; for why will ye die, O house of Israel?" (Ezekiel 33:11b). God loves to see rebellious sinners turn to him, and he orders them to do so. But the depth of sin is such that they will not, so he has ordained to call some. Those he called he also justified. Those he justified he also glorified. This is a transforming view of God.

In relation to the unbelieving world

A transforming understanding of God's effectual call frees the Christian to be a witness before the watching world. The Christian becomes God's ambassador, not God's lawyer, offering a testimony of reconciliation while leaving the rest to God. Witnessing becomes an outgrowth of love for God and for others, without the burden of having to argue someone into the kingdom, for the witness knows it is impossible to argue someone into the kingdom. There are rational proofs that God is real and has revealed himself in acts of creation and providence. There are proofs that the Bible is God's Word. The Christian should know and share these proofs for the sheer joy of giving an answer for the hope he or she has. The news is too good to keep silent, and God has invited us to be used as his witnesses throughout the world. The Christian is called to knock down the walls that separate the rationalistic human mind from God. There is a plan of salvation we are responsible to present as well as we can at each opportunity. God will judge harshly the believer who shrugs off the call to witness with the words: "Well, I'm a Calvinist, and I know the Lord will do fine in calling his people without my help."

There is a danger in Calvinism of entertaining such thoughts, but one who does so has missed the point. God chooses to work out his plan through his people when they make themselves available, and if the person with "correct theology" stands disobedient God will raise up a Finney, whose heart of hearts is stayed on the joy of seeing a lost sinner come to know abundant life.

Oh, may he use each of us, his children, to be the strong feet that follow the hound of heaven. Once he followed us; now we follow at his side. The transformed and still transforming is used as a tool of the Transformer.

What do we do about guilt?

Those whom God effectually calleth he also freely justifieth; not by infusing righteousness into them, but by pardoning their sins, and by accounting and accepting their persons as righteous: not for any thing wrought in them, or done by them, but for Christ's sake alone; not by imputing faith itself, the act of believing, or any other evangelical obedience to them, as their righteousness; but by imputing the obedience and satisfaction of Christ unto them, they receiving and resting on him and his righteousness by faith; which faith they have not of themselves, it is the gift of God. [Westminster Confession of Faith, chapter 11]

3

Forgiveness to the Uttermost

*A*bout a dozen of London's most illustrious citizens of a century ago received a singular correspondence. The envelope was quite plain, with no return address. Yet the story is told that each blanched after they tore the envelope open and read its unsigned communication. The succinct note read:

All is discovered! Flee at once!

Not one who received it thought the letter had been delivered by mistake. Each knew precisely what it meant. Some quickly found reasons to go on seaside vacations far from London as quickly as possible. And yet they were safe, for the letters were sent as a practical joke by Sir Arthur Conan Doyle, author of the Sherlock Holmes stories. Dr. Karl Menninger of the Menninger Psychiatric Clinic relates a similar story:

On a sunny September day in 1972 a plainly-dressed, stern-faced man stood on a street corner in the busy "Loop" area of downtown Chicago. The man stood there stiffly, watching each pedestrian who passed.

Then he fixed a cold eye on one, raised his hand, and pointed as the passer-by came abreast.

"Guilty!" said the man with the piercing glare.

This eerie pantomime occurred several times, Dr. Menninger said, and the effect on the people was electric. The people stopped, transfixed, to stare at their accuser for a moment. They would look down, look back at him, glance at one another, and then hurry on down the street. One of the men so arraigned was overheard saying in bewilderment: "How did he know?"

The just shall live by faith

We come to holy ground, the great central theme of redemption. The doctrine of justification broke the shackles from the soul of Martin Luther and became the very heartbeat of the Protestant Reformation. "This is the foremost pillar of religion," said John Calvin. "It is the pivotal point around which all else turns," said Geerhardus Vos. "This is the article of the creed by which the church either stands or falls," added Herman Bavinck.

> *Who shall lay any thing to the charge of God's elect? It is God that justifieth. Who is he that condemneth? It is Christ that died, yea rather, that is risen again, who is even at the right hand of God, who also maketh intercession for us.* [Romans 8:33–34]

The doctrine of justification *is* the gospel of our Lord Jesus Christ. Without at least a rudimentary understanding of the basic principle involved in this doctrine, no person will see heaven. That principle, as stated in the *Westminster Shorter Catechism* (question 33) is this:

> Justification is an act of God's free grace wherein he pardoneth all our sins, and accepteth us as righteous in his sight, only for the righteousness of Christ imputed to us, and received by faith alone.

This is the total answer for the great dilemma facing humankind: If God is truly holy and people are truly unholy, is there any hope for anyone to become acceptable to God?

The answer: "Yes, there is, but we have nothing to do with it."

Justification is an act of God—It could not be an act of a human being, because we humans are by nature offenders of God's justice. Justice had to be satisfied *for* the offended one. Only a holy and omnipotent God on his judgment throne can declare someone just.

Justification is an act of free grace—Only one reason exists as to why any person should be declared just by God—Jesus of Nazareth. No one else has earned justification; to the contrary all have earned condemnation.

Justification is an act of pardoning all sin—Pardon does not mean the criminal is declared "not guilty." It means he or she is declared "not *liable*" for the penalty fitting the crime. As we saw in looking at the character of God, each sin is an eternal affront to God's character and deserves eternal separation from God. If one crime against God remains unpardoned there is no hope of reconciliation.

Justification is an act of acceptance as righteous—
But to stand before an almighty, holy God requires
more than a blank slate. The person must become holy,
must have a positive righteousness. Justification means
that the positive righteousness of Jesus Christ's life and
sacrificial death is applied to the sinner's account. The
person is allowed to stand under a righteousness that
is not his or her own by personal character or action.
Both the absence of guilt and positive righteousness
enable God's acceptance to be just.

*Justification is an act received by faith—*God takes
something else from the sinner in lieu of positive holiness and righteousness. Belief and trust in Christ,
acceptance of Christ's sacrifice, and submission to
Christ as Lord are accepted as righteous perfection in
God's declaration that an individual is justified.

All of this may seem to be old news, but think what
it first meant to Abraham (Genesis 15:6), the writer of
Psalm 130:3–4, Isaiah (53:11), Paul (Romans 3:21–5:21),
and saints such as Martin Luther. Habakkuk 2:4 makes
the classic statement that the righteous will live, not
by righteousness, but by faith.

Guilty!

From Job (9:2b) came the cry, "How should man be just
with God?" The twentieth century has been an incon-
gruous age. Dr. Menninger's book, *Whatever Became of
Sin?* was dedicated to confronting the denial by modern
people that any such thing as sin objectively exists. We
are in a phase of denial. Yet Chicago street corners are
not the only places where guilt clings to people as if
attracted by a charge of static electricity. A psychologist
in California reported, after a study of people in mental
institutions, that those who are not there because of

organic brain dysfunction are there because of guilt. Almost without exception, guilt is responsible.

Or should we say a "*sense* of guilt" or "guilt *feelings*"? There has been great debate, especially in the twenty years since Menninger's book was published, about whether to blame objective guilt or subjective feelings of shame for the obvious psychological and spiritual trauma professionals see. Actually this debate has been in progress since Sigmund Freud theorized that neurosis is the product of harsh socialization during childhood. Freud did not believe in an absolute standard of conduct, and so he did not believe in such a thing as actual, existential guilt. But some other psychologists who do approach their study from a more or less biblical reference have come to conclude that Menninger's appeal to call sin what it is may tell only part of the story, and Freud's view that we become sick because we make mountains out of moral molehills is not altogether wrong. Christians need to be quite careful. To be transformed and transforming people of God we must deal realistically and biblically with sin and guilt—and the prescription for both. From Scripture and experience with my own guilt and the guilt of others, I would suggest that we can helpfully think of four kinds of guilt and shame:

1. *A dirtiness clings to fallen human beings.* This is actual, not just psychological, guilt. It also may be called *ultimate guilt.* In the tribunal of God, each person stands ultimately guilty. Romans 1:18–32 speaks of the picture of God that lies in the heart of every human being, a sense of what holiness and righteousness is. While humans subvert true righteousness, trading it for their own pitiful version, each has a natural awareness that they are basically unsound in life. This feeling of

not being what one was made to be is the dis-ease that accompanies the disease of depravity. Even Christians, whose sins have been taken away, can feel this dis-ease. We see the effects of this guilt in the remaining sin in our lives.

2. *Unhealthy guilt attaches to legalistically measuring self-worth by doing or being the "right thing" in our own strength.* This actually is not far from the kind of neurotic guilt that Freud saw rising from Victorian society, in which works righteousness was understood better than grace. S. Bruce Narramore believes many conservative Christians who know their salvation is a gift of God still feel a badness and the desire to be punished. Narramore believes the Christian who feels such guilt would likely describe it as: "A painful, negative emotion that somehow comes from God and is a consequence of our misbehavior, in order to motivate us to improved behavior and to serve as a form of mental punishment for our sins." Such false guilt often is a painful legacy of being brought up in an abusive home or a family where legalism, rather than true faith, measures acceptability. For others it is a desire for self-atonement and is an insidious sin in itself.

3. *Akin to these false guilt feelings is a childish pouting that lashes out irrationally at God or others through self-punishment.* Rather than maturely admitting that an action was sinful, stupid, rebellious against God, and has led to some unfortunate penalty, some people retreat into self-destructive attitudes or actions. This kind of childish guilt feeling can be complex; the person feeling it doesn't understand the rebelliousness of these inner motivations. Professional help may be needed. A philandering husband turns to alcohol after his wife leaves. An abused child grows

up to become a drug user or anorexic. A businessman whose investment collapses commits suicide. The guilt may be true or false. Its origin may not be anyone's "fault" in particular. The person becomes his or her own judge, jury, and executioner in anger at "the unfairness of it all."

4. *There is, finally, objective guilt.* A person disobeyed and feels guilty and ashamed as a result. It is good, healthy guilt, that makes the non-Christian understand the need for a Savior and can help a Christian grow. However, it certainly is frustrating and painful. Paul describes its pangs in Romans 7:7–24: "O wretched man that I am!" he shouts out in verse 24. "Who shall deliver me from the body of this death?"

The answer to all four kinds of guilt feelings is found in Romans 7:25–8:2:

I thank God through Jesus Christ our Lord. . . . There is therefore now no condemnation to them which are in Christ Jesus, who walk not after the flesh, but after the Spirit. For the law of the Spirit of life in Christ Jesus hath made me free from the law of sin and death.

The fruit of guilt

The sense of guilt that pervades our society has debilitating and disastrous effects upon human life. I am not thinking of the actual results of sin and death upon our bodies and planet, but the fruits of sin and guilt upon our spirit—the oppression that true and false guilt allow.

Anxiety

Guilt creates a sense of anxious fear. A sense of angst hangs over the heads of many people, who look over their shoulder when they walk down the street. They feel some goddess of vengeance following. Psychologists and philosophers have struggled to define this plague of the soul. Paul Tillich, for example, called it "the existential awareness of nonbeing." One of the clearest clinical descriptions, however, is one of the oldest. The Book of Job offers great insights into anxiety, depression, and guilt:

> The wicked man travaileth with pain all his days, and the number of years is hidden to the oppressor. A dreadful sound is in his ears: in prosperity the destroyer shall come upon him. He believeth not that he shall return out of darkness, and he is waited for of the sword. He wandereth abroad for bread, saying, Where is it? he knoweth that the day of darkness is ready at his hand. Trouble and anguish shall make him afraid; they shall prevail against him, as a king ready to the battle. For he stretcheth out his hand against God, and strengtheneth himself against the Almighty. He runneth upon him, even on his neck, upon the thick bosses of his bucklers [shield]. [Job 15:20–26]

> Yea, the light of the wicked shall be put out, and the spark of his fire shall not shine. The light shall be dark in his tabernacle, and his candle shall be put out with him. The steps of his strength shall be straitened, and his own counsel shall cast him down. For he is cast into a net by his own feet, and he walketh upon a snare. The gin shall take him by the heel, and the robber shall prevail against him. The snare is laid for him in the ground, and a trap for him in the way. Terrors shall make him afraid on every side, and shall drive him to his feet. His strength shall be hungerbitten, and destruction shall be ready at his side. It shall devour the strength of his skin: even the firstborn of death shall devour his strength. His confidence shall be rooted out of his taber-

nacle, and it shall bring him to the king of terrors. [Job 18:5–14]

Depression

Guilt also produces depression. In the comic strip "Li'l Abner," there was a pathetic little character who was always accompanied by his own private cloud. His little cloud was always raining. That is a good picture of the kind of depression and unhappiness that guilt creates in the human life. Guilt always rains on our parade.

The late O. Hobart Mowrer was a Christian who pioneered in trying to relate biblical faith and the findings of psychology. He saw both depression and schizophrenia as profoundly guilt related. More recently researchers have looked for some organic factors as well; still Mowrer's description has a ring of truth when he calls it "self-inflicted suffering," which would make it part of the third sort of guilt listed above (p. 59). Mowrer said that depression "looks very much like an act of 'serving time,' comparable to what happens in such other places of penance as penitentiaries where legally convicted offenders are sent."

King Saul is the classic picture of a depressive personality whose psychological illnesses were assuredly the result of personal sin. David, Saul's successor, gives a good description of the feelings inside in Psalm 38:

> There is no soundness in my flesh because of thine anger; neither is there any rest in my bones because of my sin. For mine iniquities are gone over mine head: as an heavy burden they are too heavy for me. My wounds stink and are corrupt because of my foolishness. I am troubled; I am bowed down greatly; I go mourning all the day long. . . . My heart panteth, my strength faileth me: as for the

light of mine eyes, it also is gone from me. My lovers and my friends stand aloof from my sore; and my kinsmen stand afar off. [Psalm 38:3–6, 10–11]

An inflamed conscience

Dr. John R. W. Stott, who was chaplain to the Queen of England, tells of a speaker who was addressing a Pakistani university audience concerning the Christian faith. At the conclusion of his speech, 121 people asked for private counseling. As Muslims, they did not want to know about the Trinity or the incarnation or resurrection; they wanted to know how their soiled consciences could be cleansed. Dr. Stott took a survey of his own congregation, asking: "At the time of your conversion, what was your understanding of sin and guilt?" Their responses included:

"I felt unclean."

"I felt dirty."

"I felt worthless."

"I felt like a dirty rat."

"I felt I was no good."

"I felt vile."

Is it any wonder that when guilt makes life seem unbearable, people slip into neuroses, manic-depressive states, or even schizophrenia?

A bad image

Guilt also creates a bad self-image, something we hear a great deal about today. There are many books on the subject that will never solve the problem because they don't deal with the problem of sin. As long as a person is mired down in sin and its consequent guilt, he or she is always going to feel like a louse. In fact, *louse* is a fairly accurate description. When Christians refuse to deal with sin, Satan uses that rebellion to steal away what is theirs in Christ. He simply reminds them of their louseness.

As the philosophizing opossum Pogo of the old comic strip said, "We has met the enemy and he is us!" We are our own worst enemy. Satan and his demonic horde are only created beings who cannot be omnipresent and cannot wreak all the emotional havoc with which they are blamed. Our own conscience arraigns us before the bar of justice, crying, "You are guilty! Guilty! Guilty!"

Imagine the state of the disciple Peter's emotional health after he had bragged that he would follow his Lord to the death and then denied and disowned him in cowardice. What kind of self-image problems did the risen Lord see when he looked into Peter's heart by the seashore and gently asked, "Simon, do you really love me?" (see John 21:15). Jesus, the great Physician, knew that our understanding of who we are is tied up in our affections and allegiances. Jesus alone could understand the confusion Peter felt about himself as his allegiance to Jesus had been stripped away by guilt. It would not have helped Peter for Jesus to have said: "Peter, just don't worry about it anymore." The guilt was too awesome, too real. Instead, Peter was forced to again swear his love and belongingness, once for each time of denial. This was not what Dietrich Bonhoeffer called "cheap grace" but grace that Peter now could know had been purchased with blood.

Physical illness

Time and again physicians have reported that many, even most, of their patients have more emotional than physical distress. That is not to say the illnesses are imaginary. But it is to say there is a *psychosomatic* element to them. *Psychosomatic* means that something amiss in the mind has caused something to go amiss in the body. Emotional stress has been studied in its relationship to everything from ulcers and colitis to arthritis and cancer. Even when there are underlying organic causes, the feelings of guilt may trigger them to erupt. David, perhaps after his egregious sin with Bathsheba, said, "When I kept silence, my bones waxed old through my roaring all the day long . . . my moisture is turned into the drought of summer" (Psalm 32:3–4).

Guilt and guiltiness

What truly is guilt? If you had been asked that question at the beginning of this chapter would you have responded as Narramore says the average Christian would—that guilt is "a painful, negative emotion that somehow comes from God and is a consequence of our misbehavior, in order to motivate us to improved behavior and to serve as a form of mental punishment for our sins"? Perhaps you still think of guilt as a bad feeling you get when you have done something you know to be wrong. If so, you are wrong. That is not guilt, nor what the Bible means by guilt, nor even what the law means by guilt. There is a great difference between *guilt* and *guilt feelings*. If you ask a person who is in a trauma center burn ward what "burn" is, the person may describe the searing pain experienced in his or her mind. But that pain is not why the burn patients are being treated. Their flesh has been damaged, probably several layers deep. The burn is different from the feeling of pain it inflicts in the mind.

According to the Bible, *true guilt is liability to punishment*. Suppose you have been arraigned before a court of law, charged with murder. The trial takes weeks, and the jury is out for days, and they finally reassemble.

The judge takes his place behind the bench and asks: "Ladies and gentlemen of the jury, have you reached a verdict?"

"We have, your honor," responds the foreman.

"The defendant will please rise. Ladies and gentlemen of the jury, what is your verdict?"

"We find the defendant guilty as charged."

Now there would be a catch of the breath, a closing of the throat, an increase of the pulse, an additional flow of adrenaline, perspiration, clammy hands, dizziness, a sense of nausea, and fainting. All of those would be *feelings of guilt and fear of impending punishment*. But the *liability to punishment* is the real source.

How to remove guilt and its feelings is the premier question of psychiatry and psychology. You often will hear or read that some psychiatrist now has come up with a great new insight into emotional distress. Don't believe it! According to the *Saturday Review of Literature*, there are 230 differing psychological philosophies being practiced in the United States, many of which completely contradict one another. We are fortunate that some psychology now is practiced from a Christian perspective, but not all "biblical" psychological and psychiatric models are worthy of the name; they so easily become tainted by humanistic presuppositions. Also, psychology in itself can only confront and treat guilt feelings—not the guilt itself.

Unfortunately, many psychologists simply try to deaden sensitivity—to rationalize and explain. They try to take away the pain of the burn, without healing the spiritual skin tissue that has been destroyed and is threatening to destroy the soul. One psychologist, a Dr. Gershenfeld, says that we should use words like *confused* or *mixed-up priorities*, rather than *guilt*. Should we not, as one pastoral counseling theorist suggests, deemphasize the concepts of sin and guilt, speaking, rather of a "distortion" or "inadequacy in human nature," a "sickness" that has infected the covenant relationship? By emphasizing the "judgment-justice-justification" model, he suggests, the church has been stuck in legalism when it should be offering the healing available through God's unconditional grace. There is some truth to all of these metaphors, but they fail if they suggest that sin is sickness only, and therefore not truly the person's fault. It is not legalism when Scripture says that "all have sinned, and come short of the glory of God" (Romans 3:23), and it is the individual's "fault." "There is none righteous, no, not one" (Romans 3:10). That doesn't leave out grace; rather, correct understanding of sin is a prelude to correctly understanding what grace is:

> But now the righteousness of God without the law is manifested, being witnessed by the law and the prophets; Even the righteousness of God which is by faith of Jesus Christ unto all and upon all them that believe: for there is no difference: For all have sinned, and come short of the glory of God; Being justified freely by his grace through the redemption that is in Christ Jesus. [Romans 3:21–24]

There it is, the introduction of unmerited, unearned love, directed toward those who both *feel* guilty and *are* guilty. The apostle John says if we do not acknowledge our guilt—if we claim to be innocent—"we deceive ourselves, and the truth is not in us" (1 John 1:8b). That is not neurosis. It is honest self-reflection of a kind that helps us out of our neurotic attempts to deal with sin on our own. John goes on with one of the most comforting promises in all of Scripture: "If we confess our sins, he is faithful and just to forgive us our sins, and to cleanse us from all unrighteousness" (1 John 1:9). If this is a "judgment-justice-justification" model, then I will take it over a "sickness" model any day. God has judged sin to be sin and worthy of condemnation; Christ has satisfied the just liability for punishment that is guilt; I am justified freely by grace.

A troubled young man came to see me. Years before he had broken the law and had been placed on probation. That probation was almost up, but now he had committed a relatively minor infraction, but one that called him to court before someone who well-deserved his reputation as the "hanging judge." The young offender could be sentenced to several years in prison and he was petrified. But he told me he did not want me to help him get out of it; he simply wanted me to give him something to take with him. I could do better than that. I could give him *Someone* who would go with him. He received Jesus into his life.

Jesus Christ is the perfection of justice. He is the absolutely holy and just One. His eyes are too pure to look upon iniquity. Before him if we offend in one point we are guilty of all (James 2:10–11). He will say to many, "Depart from me, ye cursed, into everlasting fire, prepared for the devil and his angels" (Matthew 25:41b). Jesus, however, is in a far different sense the "hanging judge." He is the Judge who was hanged on the tree. Jesus is the Judge who came down from behind the bench, took off his robes of glory, and went to the cross in our place.

The final answer for guilt

In Romans 8:33–34 Paul asks the most important questions one oppressed by guilt will ever hear:
>   *Question:* Who will bring any charge against those whom God has chosen?
>   *Answer:* It is God.
>   *Question:* Who is he that condemns?

Answer: No one for the Christian. The Judge who is Jesus Christ, who intercedes for me.

Question: Paul, is this God the same God who also justifies?

Answer: It is the very same.

Question: Paul, is this the hanging judge—the one who died and was raised to life? Is this the same judge who is at the right hand of God and is interceding for us?

Answer: Yes, that is the One.

All this happens through a process called justification. God in Jesus Christ freely justifies; he pronounces, accepts, and treats as just one who is no longer liable for punishment. The *Westminster Confession* makes an important distinction at this point. The law has been disobeyed, and God does not justify by simply waving his hand and saying, "All is well. I will forget about the broken law and infuse you with righteousness." God would not be just if he did that. The skeptic who joked that God would forgive him "because that is God's business" will be sadly disappointed. Rather, said the Westminster divines, God "accepts sinners as righteous" who have come under the blood of Christ. Charles Wesley described it as having an interest in Christ's blood:

> And can it be that I should gain
> An interest in the Savior's blood?
> Died He for me, who caused His pain?
> For me, who Him to death pursued?
> Amazing love! How can it be
> That Thou, my God, shouldst die for me?

The *Confession* says that when I stand before the Judge, he looks at me and sees nothing but Christ's obedience and the satisfaction of the law's demands. "For

the wages of sin is death; but the gift of God is eternal
life through Jesus Christ our Lord" (Romans 6:23; see
also Ephesians 1:7). All the sinner adds is faith, believing "on him that raised up Jesus our Lord from the
dead" (Romans 4:24). "If thou shalt confess with thy
mouth the Lord Jesus, and shalt believe in thine heart
that God raised him from the dead, thou shalt be
saved" (Romans 10:9). No, Paul says, we do not really
even add the faith. God gives us the faith to place in
Christ—something we would never do on our own
(Ephesians 2:8–9; Philippians 1:29). Wesley's hymn continues:

> No condemnation now I dread,
> Jesus, and all in Him, is mine!
> Alive in Him, my living Head,
> And clothed in righteousness divine,
> Bold I approach the eternal throne,
> And claim the crown, through Christ my own.
> Amazing love! How can it be
> That Thou, my God, shouldst die for me?

This is forgiveness to the uttermost. Condemnation
is replaced with a crown.

What justification is not

We have said a great deal about what justification does
in freeing us from the penalty for sin. We should also
say what it is not and what it will not do.

Justification does not change our hearts, souls, or
lives one whit. It has to do with what God declares
about our guilt, and what he sees when he looks at us
in Christ. The declaration that we are righteous is
entirely external to us. Indeed, God does internally

change us, but that is *regeneration* and *sanctification*. The implication of this is that the problem with sin and guilt in our lives will not go away once we trust in Christ and are reborn. You are no better after you are justified than before. You are not one bit holier. We can not separate justification from sanctification.

Yet its significance in changing us is fantastic in two senses.

First, no one who understands justification will ever again try to cling to good works for salvation. John Gerstner has described the plight of the proud man in this way:

> Christ has done everything necessary for his salvation. Nothing now stands between the sinner and God but the sinner's "good works." Nothing can keep him from Christ but his delusion that he does not need him—that he has good works of his own that can satisfy God. If men will only be convinced that they have no righteousness that is not as filthy rags; if men will see that there is none that doeth good, no, not one; if men will see that all are shut up under sin—then there will be nothing to prevent their everlasting salvation. All they need is need. All they must have is nothing. All that is required is acknowledged guilt. But, alas, sinners cannot part with their "virtues." They have none that are not imaginary, but they are real to them. So grace becomes unreal. The real grace of God they spurn in order to hold on to the illusory virtues of their own. Their eyes fixed on a mirage, they will not drink real water. They die of thirst in the midst of an ocean of Grace.

Right now you are clinging to something in your hope that you are acceptable to yourself and to God. There will be one day, said Jesus, a great wedding feast (Matthew 22:10–13). All who come will have on beautiful white garments—the righteousness of Christ. But

one man comes into the wedding feast in Jesus' parable who does not have on a wedding garment. Likely
he supposes himself to be dressed in his Sunday best,
dressed in morality, money given to charity, com-
mandment keeping, Golden-rule living, and general
"niceness." Unfortunately, the guest doesn't truly see
his clothing very well. To the king he is filthy, foul-
smelling, and louse-infested. "Friend," the king asked,
"how camest thou in hither not having a wedding garment?" Jesus said the man was speechless. He had no
defense. "Then said the king to the servants, Bind him
hand and foot, and take him away, and cast him into
outer darkness; there shall be weeping and gnashing
of teeth."

Second, justification should transform the sinner's
self-image. The great malady of our age is conquered.
We have been forgiven. This is fact, not surmise. Someone from an Evangelism Explosion calling team asks:
"Suppose that you were to die tonight and stand before
God and he were to say to you, 'Why should I let you
into my heaven?' What would you say?" What a feeling it is to know that you could answer: "I am declared
just, only in the blood of Jesus Christ, my Savior and
Lord."

With that out of the way, I have peace with God and
access to God and hope of glory (Romans 5:1–2). Peace,
access, and hope are the great needs of the age of guilt,
the great antidotes to depression and feelings of guilt.
If we cling to Christ we have peace, access, and hope.

Therefore, the dirtiness that clings to us as ultimate
guilt also is ultimately powerless. As fallen human
beings we will die, and death will take us into the glory
of God's presence. Original sin's guilt is taken care of
on the cross. Cling to Christ, and the depression that
comes from the human condition loses its power to
oppress.

Therefore, the guilt of trying to do the right thing and failing is absolutely powerless to oppress. If salvation is a gift of God and not of works, the filthiness of a person's own good works truly is irrelevant. What I do, I do to the glory of God, and he will accept it as praise on that basis. Cling to Christ and the need for self-punishment loses its power to oppress.

Therefore, the childish desire to lash out at oneself, God, or others can be replaced by mature dealing with mistakes. An adult way has been made for the Christian to be forgiven of sin. Emotional bondage loses its power to oppress.

Therefore, objective guilt is gone, so far as God is concerned. Yes, the person will do wrong and be liable to chastisement by God and civil/criminal/social penalties imposed by society. However, what penalties I must pay in the flesh for sin are God's disciplining hand to help me be more like Christ (Hebrews 12:4–13). Unpleasant though they be, at least I know they will be used to strengthen and further sanctify me. I am forgiven to the uttermost and guilt has no oppressive power over me.

What does it mean that Christians are adopted?

All those that are justified God vouchsafeth, in and for his only Son Jesus Christ, to make partakers of the grace of adoption; by which they are taken into the number, and enjoy the liberties and privileges of the children of God; have his name put upon them; receive the Spirit of adoption; have access to the throne of grace with boldness; are enabled to cry, Abba, Father; are pitied, protected, provided for, and chastened by him as by a father; yet never cast off, but sealed to the day of redemption, and inherit the promises as heirs of everlasting salvation. [Westminster Confession of Faith, chapter 12]

4

Abba, Daddy

They had studied for years. They had planned, designed, tinkered, built, attempted, and failed. Then on a December morning on the sand dunes of Kitty Hawk, North Carolina, Orville and Wilbur Wright broke the shackles of gravity and lifted humanity upward in the first powered flight. They knew the significance of their victory and immediately sent a telegram to their sister Katherine. She ran right down to the newspaper office and showed it to the editor.

"We have actually flown 120 feet. Will be home for Christmas," the telegram said. In his hands that editor held the scoop of the year, the story of the decade, perhaps the most significant news of the new century. The editor read it carefully and smiled.

"Well, well! How nice. The boys will be home for Christmas," he said.

He had planned and designed before the first star burst into flame to light the darkness. Then, when the world was in the grips of sin and distress, at just the right moment, the triune God undertook a flight far greater than that of Orville and Wilbur's. Christ flew through the galaxies, from the mansions of glory, into the filth of a cave used as a stable. Millions have heard of that flight and said, in the midst of their slavery to fear, "Well, well. Jesus was born at Bethlehem. That's sweet."

Others have looked at the same event and become more frightened of it. "Well, well. Now don't talk about such things. We want to stress the brotherhood of all people instead of one set of narrow religious interests."

As a result of both answers, our society is wracked by what Romans 8:15 calls a spirit of fear, when a Spirit of sonship with God would break the shackles of fear and lift humanity. That sounds like the greatest news of this or any other century, for verses 16 and 17 continue: "The Spirit itself beareth witness with our spirit, that we are the children of God: And if children, then heirs; heirs of God, and joint-heirs with Christ; if so be that we suffer with him, that we may be also glorified together." In Christ the believer has been *adopted* by God.

> *For ye have not received the spirit of bondage again to fear; but ye have received the Spirit of adoption, whereby we cry, Abba, Father. The Spirit itself beareth witness with our spirit, that we are the children of God: And if children, then heirs; heirs of God, and joint-heirs with Christ.*
> [Romans 8:15–17a]

That implies wonderful things. Already we see one wonder. We need no longer be slaves to fear. We shall see that it also denies universalism, the great error of our time.

Fitting adoption into the big picture

We have seen two great covenants or promises that were given by God, the covenant of life, and the covenant of grace. The Bible speaks of being adopted as children of God within the covenant of grace. Adoption returns to us something that was lost after the covenant of life was broken.

God had created the world and made Adam in a perfect, sinless state when he gave him the covenant of life. While this covenant was operating we see the wonderful picture of fellowship between creature and Creator (Genesis 1:27–2:25). While any analogy falls short, the closeness depicted by Scripture resembles the intimacy of a parent-young child relationship— the relationship of a parent and child when both are functioning in their proper roles and intimate communication and love flow back and forth easily. The child feels most comfortable when in touch with the parent. There is no desire to break away or rebel.

The promise of the covenant of life was based on a probationary command. Adam had one command he was to keep to show his obedience and devotion to his God. If he kept it he would earn for himself and all his children eternal blessedness, bliss, and peace. He would, through this command, be enabled to fulfil the purpose for which people were created: to glorify God and enjoy him forever. However, he chose to rebel, plunging the human race into sin and fear, death and misery.

Why should God care to set in place his second covenant—the covenant of grace? God certainly could have let men and women go their own way, or wiped them out and started over. Instead, he offered another way to eternal life, a way that took into account the true condition of the fallen, who "glorified him not as God, neither were thankful; but became vain in their imaginations, and their foolish heart was darkened" (Romans 1:21). Left alone, the human heart opposes God. No human heart understands or appreciates the things of the Spirit (Romans 3:11).

Therefore, God determined to select a great mass of men and women out of every nation and language. These were individually chosen before even one of them was born, in fact before the fall into sin itself had occurred (Ephesians 1:4–6; Revelation 5:9). Into the hearts of each of these dead individuals he sends his Spirit, irresistibly, unfailingly drawing them to him. The Spirit makes their hearts and minds new, brings their souls, dead with sin, to life in Christ (Ephesians 2:1–10). They come most willingly, made willing by his grace.

Still, none of this would have been possible if the guilt-price of sin had not been paid. To purchase salvation for all who come to him, so that he might remain the just Judge, God gave his unique Son, a part of himself, to pay for their transgressions. At just the right time in each life, God sent his Holy Spirit to effectually call them through their individual experiences and background. In some great outpourings of grace in history, hundreds, even thousands have laid their lives at the cross in a brief time. This still was no mass production operation of the Spirit. In each heart the Spirit worked through that mind and those life experiences to individually relate the gospel to them in their situation and cultural background. By understanding through the Bible and renewal through the Spirit a dead mind leaps to life, a soul is reborn, a will is made malleable. After hearing God's voice and knock at the door, each sinner says in his or her own experience, "Come in, my Beloved." After receiving trusting faith from God as a gift, the individual is justified (declared to be righteous) on the basis of that faith God has given.

At every point salvation is from God. If you want the theological term for all of these steps God has taken the sinner through toward himself, it is called the *ordo salutis*—"the way of salvation." While these steps may take some time, or they may seem to happen over an instant, the *ordo salutis* is a logical progression for us to use in understanding the process. However, the steps of this path are not yet completed, though even some of the great Christian thinkers stopped at this point, neglecting entirely what happens in *adoption*. Scripture has some things to say about it, though, and the writers of the *Westminster Confession* were careful to give it its due place in how we understand what God does for us. We are predestined or chosen by God so that we may be adopted as children of God, brothers and sisters of Christ. This is the ultimate blessing of the Christian life.

Child of God, or of Satan?

Adoption is also the point at which we confront a serious error—*universalism*. The universalist says that somehow, somewhere, sometime, every one of God's creatures will ultimately arrive in paradise. Universalism has been strongly preached from many pulpits by those who are so caught up in the idea that God is love that they abhor the thought that anyone could be eternally punished in hell. Yet the Bible plainly teaches that those who reject Christ will be forever separated from God. Jesus Christ himself made it plain:

> Enter ye in at the strait [narrow] gate: for wide is the gate, and broad is the way, that leadeth to destruction, and many there be which go in thereat: Because strait is the gate, and narrow is the way, which leadeth unto life, and few there be that find it. [Matthew 7:13–14]

> When the Son of man shall come in his glory, and all the holy angels with him, then shall he sit upon the throne of his glory: And before him shall be gathered all nations: and he shall separate them one from another, as a shepherd divideth his sheep from the goats: And he shall set the sheep on his right hand, but the goats on the left. . . . And these shall go away into everlasting punishment: but the righteousness into life eternal. [Matthew 25:31–33, 46]

> And if thine eye offend thee, pluck it out: it is better for thee to enter into the kingdom of God with one eye, than having two eyes to be cast into hell fire: Where their worm dieth not, and the fire is not quenched. [Mark 9:47–48]

> He that believeth on the Son hath everlasting life: and he that believeth not the Son shall not see life; but the wrath of God abideth on him. [John 3:36]

Universalism impinges upon the doctrine of adoption when universalists speak of the "fatherhood of God and the brotherhood of man." It sounds very loving and spiritual to sing, with the once popular chorus, "With God as our Father, brothers all are we. Let me walk with my brother, in perfect harmony." Many believe that sentiment to be from the Bible, but the idea that God is Father of all and that all are brothers and sisters is utterly foreign to the Scriptures. This false unity is true to the ideals of humanism, not Christianity. Jesus looked at the religious people of his day, who thought themselves children of Abraham, and said, "Ye are of your father the devil, and the lusts of your father ye will do" (John 8:44a). Paul takes an equally pessimistic view of those outside the kingdom of God: "And you hath he quickened, who were dead in trespasses and sins; Wherein in time past ye walked according to the course of this world, according to the prince of the power of the air, the spirit that now worketh in the children of disobedience" (Ephesians 2:1–2).

The state of the one who has not accepted Christ is hardly one of brotherhood with those who have. The disobedient child of the devil is under God's anger; his or her only connection with the kingdom of God is enmity. True connection with God comes only as we are transformed from the kingdom of darkness into the kingdom of God's dear Son: "But as many as received him, to them gave he power to become the sons of God, even to them that believe on his name" (John 1:12).

Childhood and citizenship

Can anyone *become* something he or she *already is*? Of course not. Romans 9:8 makes it clear that it is not the natural children who are God's children, but it is the children of the promise who are regarded as Abraham's (Romans 9:8). Abraham's offspring? It was Abraham who was declared righteous (justified) by his faith. He looked forward to the coming of a Savior for his sins. Now we can look back on the cross (rather than forward as did Abraham), but we are declared righteous in the same way he was and through justification become the true children of Abraham. The justified ones, as children of Abraham, are children of God. This is not a promise to children of the flesh but children of the Spirit. In fact, in a spiritual sense the children of the Spirit are to stand apart:

> Wherefore come out from among them, and be ye separate, saith the Lord, and touch not the unclean thing; and I will receive you, And will be a Father unto you, and ye shall be my sons and daughters, saith the Lord Almighty. [2 Corinthians 6:17–18]

The deception of the devil may be that all people are the children of God, that God is Father of all, but this is not the teaching of Scripture.

To be perfectly accurate we should notice three meanings for the term *sons/children of God* in Scripture. First, when God made Adam he was the son of God. That special status was obliterated in the fall into sin. Second, those in Christ are *adopted* children of God by receiving him as Savior and believing on him (John 1:12). Third, in its most restrictive and unique sense, the term applies to Jesus Christ, the eternal second person of the Trinity, who has forever been the Son of God (see book 1, p. 111).

Adam was both son and subject. He was a member of the divine kingdom and of the divine household. God, to him, was Sovereign and Lord; he also was Father and Friend. If Adam had obeyed, we would all have an eternal citizenship in the kingdom of God and eternal sonship in the house of God. But Adam sinned against the magisterial favor of the King and against the paternal regard of the Father. In one act he sinned in both ways. As a result he became an outlawed citizen and a disinherited son. Therefore, all his children are born out of relationship with the righteous Judge and the benevolent Father. The human condition was described succinctly by Robert Webb, who said concerning Adam and all his natural children:

> There was, there could be, there ought to have been, but one denouement to such a situation—a child with a heart so perverted ought to have been excluded. God dismissed him. Today he has neither the right nor spirit of a child. He is legally disowned because he is morally bad. He is ungoverned, because he is ungovernable. He has thrown off his Father's authority, because he has cast away his Father's disposition. Moral gravitation has naturally and logically carried him into that fellowship where the outraged sensibilities of his Father have justly consigned him. Parental discipline has dealt with him according to the demands and desires of his own degenerate nature. He has been permitted to have his wilful way; and the misery of his course will be the just retribution of his heady and impertinent career. He is a child of Satan; therefore a "child of wrath."

This dreadful condition needs a twofold remedy. As proscribed citizen and disinherited child, each person must be restored to legal citizenship and be recovered into the bosom and household of the Father. This double remedy is clearly stated in Scripture. On one hand, the problem of citizenship is dealt with by justification. In justification the transgressed law of God is fulfilled by Christ and the penalty paid by him. The sinner is clothed in the righteousness of Christ and restored to the kingdom of God. Sonship is taken care of in adoption. The saved sinner is adopted into the family of God and restored to his household.

Obviously adoption is closely related to justification and to the overall process of being born again (regenerated). Not only must the child be restored to a filial disposition; the child must also be given a filial nature, the nature of a child. The spiteful attitude of natural humanity says to the parents: "I hate you; I never want to lay eyes on you again. I couldn't care less what you have done for me." The regenerated person has a new heart and nature and acts like a child, in keeping with the new rights and privileges of son and daughterhood.

The errors of universalism

Let us compare that with the theology of the father-hood of God/brotherhood of man. This is a new religion of paternalism. It is interesting that universalism should rise in the twentieth century, at a time the Western European and North American governments have been exercising a more paternalistic attitude toward citizens. People have come to believe they have a right to be taken care of. In keeping with that, God must be the Father of everyone.

Universalism fails to realize God's absolute perfection. It would be unfair for him to leave out anyone. He did not create people because he was lonely; he existed in perfect fellowship with himself. God created humans for his own glory.

Universalism fails to understand the difference between divine government and divine discipline; between the rule of a Sovereign and the rule of a Father. A sovereign-state ruler exercises justice and punishes the rebellious. A father operates out of love, chastening instead of punishing. There is a great difference between chastening and punishing. Punishment is retrospective—it looks back to the broken law and is not done to make the criminal better. A lawbreaker is punished because the law has been violated. Chastisement is prospective—it looks forward to future behavior. It is given to correct a fault, to make the child better. An electric chair makes no one better. It may make society better since one of the reasons for justice is the protection of society; but the reason for chastening is to make a better child.

Universalism denies the need for an atonement. It reduces the Bible to the story of the prodigal son, where the father embraces the son without payment for sins. But that is the nature of fatherly discipline. All the father requires is repentance and evidence of a desire to do better. So people who suppose this to be the way of salvation believe that if a person merely wants to do better in the future, all will be well. This is to suppose a murderer who has been given a life sentence rattles the bars and says to the warden: "Warden, I've had a change of heart. You will be delighted to know that I'm sorry about the whole thing. I've decided I shouldn't have killed all those people. Please tell the jailer to open the cage and let me out because I'll never do that again."

The universalist fails to understand that only identification with Jesus Christ can make a sinner both a member of God's kingdom and of his family. Jesus was the suffering Servant who remained subject to the King—obedient to God in all his ways. Jesus paid the penalty as the Servant; thus God restores him to legal citizenship in the kingdom. Jesus is also the very Son of God because it takes the Son by filial obedience to restore the sinful, disobedient son to a filial relation. So Christ the suffering Son provides for us both justification's restoration to the kingdom and adoption's reclamation into the family.

Gifts from the Father

The *Westminster Confession of Faith* notes that we should think of adoption as growing from justification.

"All those that are justified God vouchsafeth, in and for his only Son Jesus Christ, to make partakers of the grace of adoption." To vouchsafe means to condescend to give. Adam's and Eve's original rights and privileges were based upon a wonderful act of condescension that was possible because they stood as righteous in God's sight. God can vouchsafe nothing for those he cannot look on because of their sin. This was the Westminster writers' way of saying that adoption presents the proof that the guilt of sin has been removed. Restoration has occurred, so reclamation is possible. Our God can bend down to pick us up and hold us again in his arms. What is vouchsafed for those who are taken into the number and enjoy the liberties and privileges of the adopted?

God gives them his name. I have always felt a special admiration for those who are willing to become foster parents. Foster parents, as the state usually defines them, are parents who temporarily take over parenthood for children who cannot remain with their natural parents. Some sort of intervention is required to get the child's own family functioning again. It is not the nurturing environment that child needs for the moment. The child goes to live with the foster parents for weeks, even months; yet when the child returns to its birth parents the foster relationship is broken. The foster mother and father must say good-bye and put away the special affections they may have enjoyed for this child. The foster parent can not give the child a new name. There can be no permanent relationship signified by the change in name. In biblical times a change in God's relationship with a person often accompanied a new name. *Abram* and *Sarai* became *Abraham* and *Sarah*; *Jacob* became *Israel.* In the New Testament *Simon* the fisherman became *Peter* the "rock."

God gives them his Spirit. Every child has something of the nature of his father and mother within him.

There is a genetic connection. Our hair may be the same color, our build the same type, and some natural affinities and abilities may be similar. Also, by virtue of being together through those formative years of childhood, children who have had a strong bond with their parents often seem to have a sort of kinship in spirit. This may return in adulthood even if there has been a tumultuous breaking away time when the parents and the child see almost nothing the same way at all.

But with God this spiritual connection is an actual Spirit connection. It is like the genetic link between blood relatives in that the Spirit of God takes up residence in the Christian's inner being. Holiness becomes part of who we are as new creatures. Those that become the children of God have a new desire for holiness, and even wisdom, which is one of the attributes of God. God gives to every child of his a certain divine wisdom, a wisdom of things eternal, which the world, regardless of its knowledge or education, knows nothing about. We receive the divine nature.

Singer Amy Grant expressed what this ought to mean for the Christian in a song entitled "Father's Eyes." The theme of the song is that we may have many traces of our family in our lives, but the Christian should most desire to see one's self and other people through the eyes of God's perspective.

The Holy Spirit is just as much a part of who God is as the Father and Son. This Spirit of adoption gives us gifts and direction from God and intercedes with God on our behalf.

Therefore we have access to the throne of grace with boldness. One lasting impression of John F. Kennedy's presidency was that of his toddler son's constant access to his father. Heads of state might be gathered in the oval office, yet on the rug in the center of the room little John was absorbed in his toys, knowing that daddy's lap was available if he wanted it. As the child of the King of the universe, we may push our toy trucks and other trappings of earthly preoccupation around on the floor, knowing we are in the presence of *Abba* and his lap is not too big to climb upon. And while a parent may not always understand what needs are expressed by those sniffling, incoherent cries of anguish, the Holy Spirit is our Translator, explaining what we want and what we really need.

God allows us Abba *intimacy.* Within our relationship we are pitied, protected, provided for, and chastened by him as by a father; yet never cast off. How sad a commentary on the godlessness of society that we have to be a little cautious in describing God as a Father. For many people, a father is the last thing they want God to be if that makes God what their own father was. We have come to the point where a minority of children know a stable father-child relationship. Father tends to be abusive or weak or absent. So God as father seems an ogreish, self-centered, or irrelevant image.

God has made us heirs. All that the Father has will one day be ours. "All things are yours," said the apostle Paul—the things in this world and the things to come. I am the heir of God, included in the will—only a living inheritance from a living Father. The New Testament of our Lord and Savior Jesus Christ is the will of God. And all who will receive Jesus Christ have their names in the Lamb's Book of Life and are heirs of God.

God gives us access to his home. Jesus has gone to prepare, in his Father's house, a place for each Christian. We are brought into the family of God, given his name, and made heirs by an act of God's grace. We also have the promise that we have his Spirit within us. He pities us as a Father, provides for all our needs, watches over us, defends us from our enemies, and one day will take us to our mansion in glory—the mansion he has prepared for us. How wonderful it is that because of the Spirit of adoption we can look up into the face of God, whom many fear, and say, "*Abba*, Father" (Romans 8:15b).

Love without measure

I once pointed out to a Jehovah's Witness that the New World translation is not correct when it includes in the New Testament the word *Jehovah* as the name of God, since it does not appear once in the New Testament Greek text. *Theos*, the generic Greek word for god is used often, but never the word *Yahweh* or, as the King James Version expresses it, *Jehovah*. "Why would God not use his Name in the New Testament?" the person asked. I cannot answer for God, but I have an idea as to the reason. When my little girl, Jennifer, was about five years old she passed through a phase when she began to call her mother and father by our first names— Anne and Jim. She heard others use these words and didn't see why she couldn't use them too. After a few weeks of this I sat her on my knee and said, "Jennifer, darling, there are thousands of people in this world who can call me Jim, but there is no other person on this earth who can call me 'daddy' except you, and to you, Jennifer, my name is Daddy." So also God revealed his name in the Old Testament as *Yahweh*—Jehovah, the Ever-Living One. But in the New Testament, when we are given the Spirit of adoption and brought into that intimate relationship as sons and daughters of God, we can look up into the face of our Father and say, "*Abba*," a diminutive of the Aramaic word for "father" that means, essentially, "daddy."

You may feel bruised and battered by life. You may feel all alone and cast down. If you are a parent you know something of the love of a parent for a child, the love that reaches out after a child even in its waywardness, a love that reaches out to a child in pain, a love that reaches after a child who has deserted the family, a love that never lets go. All of that tender compassion of a human parent's love is but the faintest shadow of the infinite love of God, which knows no measure—a love that could never let us go. When we become children of God we enter into that parental love of God. Have you come to the place when you can say, "I'm a child of the King. I can go to God as *Abba*"? If so then you know how transforming love can be. If not, then you can experience it—not the sickly passed-around love of the universalist's god, but the God who sets his love on those who are justified in Christ.

What is a sanctified life?

They who are effectually called and regenerated, having a new heart and a new spirit created in them, are further sanctified, really and personally, through the virtue of Christ's death and resurrection, by his Word and Spirit dwelling in them; the dominion of the whole body of sin is destroyed, and the several lusts thereof are more and more weakened and mortified, and they more and more quickened and strengthened, in all saving graces, to the practice of true holiness, without which no man shall see the Lord. [Westminster Confession of Faith, chapter 13]

5

The Glint of Gold

When I was a seminary student I heard a story, told by a preacher from Canada, that I shall never forget:

One day a young woman in the church came to him for counsel. She had a terrible situation at home. She lived with a man who was an ogre. She got along fine with her husband, but her father-in-law had come to live with them. He was mean and bitter. He had a vile mouth and a blasphemous tongue, and it cut loose on her every time she did anything that displeased him in the slightest.

Now this woman had some spirit herself and was not about to be used as anyone's doormat. So when he gave it to her she gave it right back. Only later she always felt bad about it. Her anger hadn't accomplished anything, and these continual altercations were hard on everyone. She wondered what she should do.

The pastor was new to the ministry, and this problem sounded like it was beyond his meager store of wisdom. But he did have one idea.

"What is a food your father-in-law loves to eat?" the pastor asked.

The woman was taken aback by the question. She thought, "I knew I shouldn't have come to such a young

---

man for advice. What does he know about anything?"
But after a moment she answered that her father-in-
law loved fudge.

"Next time he gets angry with you, make him some
fudge," said the pastor.

She left, despairing of preachers not yet dry behind
the ears. A few days later the next explosion occurred.
She was going about her business in the kitchen. It was
a wintry day, and this ugly man was sitting with his
feet propped up on the
potbelly stove. He had
gout in one foot, and the
heat helped. There he sat,
his feet up and his hands
folded around an opulent
belly, when she acciden-
tally splashed hot water
on his hurting foot. He
explained the full depth
of his feelings in the most
colorful language. Her
blood pressure rose until
red reached the tip of her
ears. She was ready to
blow him off his seat
when she remembered
the preacher's insane
advice. She stopped,
counted to ten, turned
around, and started to
make fudge.

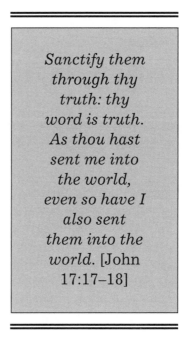

Sanctify them through thy truth: thy word is truth. As thou hast sent me into the world, even so have I also sent them into the world. [John 17:17–18]

Meanwhile the bear settled back into his den, folded
his hands, and went back to sleep. He slept while she
mixed the ingredients, made the fudge, and cooled it.
She cut some pieces, put them on a plate, and stuck the
plate under her father-in-law's nose. One eye opened,

then the other. He looked down at the plate of fudge, but he didn't move for a long time. He sat there thinking about his hurtful words and the fudge, his blasphemies and the fudge. A large tear slid down his cheek and dampened one of the pieces. He slowly slid out of the chair onto his knees, put his arms around her waist, and said, "Daughter, I want you to forgive a mean and ornery old man."

That day she had the joy of leading her father-in-law to the Lord.

Fudge grace

Wouldn't it be great if all interpersonal problems could be solved with a plate of fudge? Perhaps more could than we might imagine. The secret ingredient wasn't in the fudge, however. Something more intangible and mysterious was going on in two hearts. In the father-in-law's soul the Spirit of God drew the old man and made him willing. This transformation used the Word of God that had been placed in his mind in the past and the words his daughter-in-law used to share the gospel. This was God's grace.

The Spirit also used "fudge grace." Through the plate of an undeserved gift of grace the old man saw his own sin in stark contrast. Words of bitterness that had long been a habitual way of life were seen in all of their true ugliness against the backdrop of an act of sacrifice. He wasn't simply told about Jesus' sacrifice; he would have scoffed at such words from a daughter-in-law who traded insult for insult. Rather, he saw a demonstration of Jesus' sacrifice mirrored in a life.

It is like a prospector who fills a pan with riverbed rock and dirt. Most of what he pans is worthless sludge and splashes over the side of the pan. But occasionally the sunlight hits something small but sparklingly different in the pan. That sparkle makes the prospector's heart beat faster, for this is what his back-breaking labor and nights sleeping in the cold have been about. This is the glint of gold.

The Holy Spirit was also at work in the woman. Remember her reaction to the pastor. His advice only applied Scripture. Had she read those verses for herself she might never have connected them with the man whose feet were warming on her stove. Yet now the Holy Spirit took Scripture, mediated in the willing mind of the pastor, and gently applied it like sandpaper. The Spirit molded, smoothed, and shaped her mind. Fudge was not the natural reaction to abuse, but it was God's way. A growing child of God put off anger and became a vessel of love. That is the fudge grace called sanctification that God promises to every believer, the transforming power to be holy like our Lord.

The doctrine behind the life

The exceedingly important doctrine of sanctification reaches us right where we are. It has to do with life as we are living it now. Sanctification seems such a simple matter—merely living the Christian life. But not one church member in ten has the foggiest notion of what the biblical doctrine of sanctification really is. This is partly why there is so little true sanctification in the church. Sanctification is a doctrine as well as a life.

Sanctification is closely related to justification—so closely that the two often are confused. Though they can never be separated, they must be distinguished. One way to make the distinction is to place the definitions side by side as they were set out by the writers of the *Westminster Shorter Catechism,* questions 33 and 35:

What is justification?

Justification is an act of God's free grace, wherein he pardoneth all our sins, and accepteth us as righteous in his sight, only for the righteousness of Christ imputed to us, and received by faith alone.

What is sanctification?

Sanctification is the work of God's free grace, whereby we are renewed in the whole man after the image of God, and are enabled more and more to die unto sin and live unto righteousness.

Act and process

The first difference is that justification is an act; sanctification is a process. Justification takes place once for all and is complete and perfect. Sanctification is imperfect. It is a long process that lasts from the moment Christian life begins until the moment earthly life ends.

Courtroom and hospital

Second, justification is entirely external, while sanctification works in us. Jesus satisfied the penalty for our sins. We had nothing to do with his sacrifice on the cross. Justification is the act of God as Judge declaring us righteous in his sight through the death of Christ. We had nothing to do with that declaration. We are entered into the book of the kingdom of God. We did not write our names down. Nothing happens in justification inside us at all.

Sanctification takes the metaphor from the court-room to the hospital. A trauma victim enters on a cart and is immediately wheeled to surgery. The condition is stabilized, but other treatments and therapy may take time. Sanctification begins with the work of a Surgeon within our persons. We are made holy before God when we are justified and clothed with Christ's righteousness. But then comes a lifelong patient-Physician relationship. We are actively involved in becoming what God has declared us to be. This process is intimately connected with our thoughts and actions. To change the image slightly, we are saints under construction—a hard-hat work site.

Guilt and corruption

The third difference involves God's purposes in the act of justification and the work of sanctification. They deal with two very different aspects of sin. If you do not distinguish these aspects you will have difficulty understanding Christian theology.

The first aspect of sin is its guilt, what we have described as liability (see pp. 65–68). The lawbreaker in the civil realm is liable to punishment. This is guilt. Anyone who sins against the law of God is liable to punishment. But justification reverses this liability. The righteousness of Christ has been imputed to the sinner. God tolerates no unrighteousness. If you have been made acceptable your account stands spotless so far as God is concerned. You are clothed with the garment of grace. In your flesh you may pay the penalty for sins committed. In God's sight no penalty is due.

The second aspect of sin is its corrupting power. In this aspect lies the filth with which sin stains our personalities, minds, and actions. Sanctification is the operation of doing away with the corruption. This is not done by imputing Christ's righteousness to us. It is accomplished by infusing Christ's holiness into us.

Anyone who has bitten into a rotten or wormy apple has experienced the nauseating reality of corruption. After a few days a corrupt apple need not be tasted for its problem to be identified. A glance reveals the brown, wrinkling decay, a touch the squishy unwholesomeness. Keep it around a little longer and a strange odor pervades its surroundings. Rottenness no longer needs to be tasted, seen, or touched. Likewise, humankind stinks to high heaven. Not a flattering thought. From the top of our heads to the soles of our feet there is nothing but corruption within. In the English language *holiness* relates to the word *whole*—as in wholeness, soundness, oneness. We know how to make a good apple rotten, but only God can make a rotten apple sound. A corrupting human apple can become whole again by connection to the Tree, the Source of soundness. Jesus used a slightly different picture to make the same point, that wholeness (and holiness) occurs only through connection:

> I am the true vine, and my Father is the husbandman . . . Abide in me, and I in you. As the branch cannot bear fruit of itself, except it abide in the vine; no more can ye, except ye abide in me. I am the vine, ye are the branches: He that abideth in me, and I in him, the same bringeth forth much fruit: for without me ye can do nothing. If a man abide not in me, he is cast forth as a branch, and is withered; and men gather them, and cast them into the fire, and they are burned. [John 15:1, 4–6]

Take an apple off of the tree, leave it around long enough, and rottenness results. If we are severed from the Vine we will become corrupt. Holiness is an attribute of God alone, and holiness in anyone or anything in this world exists only in relation to God. The holiness of God flows into it in some way.

The call to connection

The justified Christian has been removed from liability. But establishing the vital vine-branch connection is only the beginning. While God accepts the new believer, the connection is weak because of the ongoing effects of the sin-nature: "Thou art of purer eyes than to behold evil, and canst not look on iniquity" (Habakkuk 1:13). God is intolerant of *all* sin, in the unbeliever and the believer. If you have never truly experienced intimacy with God, and I believe few Christians enjoy that experience, it likely is because much of your life remains contrary to the holiness of God. Your rebellion remains an abomination. The vine-branch connection remains weak. True holiness needs to replace remaining unholiness that God hates. Sanctification is the answer.

But the need for sanctification may raise a few questions:

1. Why, if the penalty for sin has been taken care of, must I be so concerned with holiness?
2. On the other hand, when Jesus talks about remaining connected to him in John 15 he warns about branches being cut off and thrown into the fire. Can I lose my salvation if the process of sanctification doesn't "take"?
3. But sanctification is a work of God. So isn't it really out of my hands?

Why be concerned?

Our Father is God of the universe, holy and perfect, omniscient and omnipotent. I should be careful about making him angry if I am his child. He is a loving Father, but he is no wimp. And he has made a world in which sin has consequences, some of them drastic. Ananias and Sapphira were early church members who thought they could keep God as a convenient fire escape (Acts 5:1–11). We are not told whether this man and wife had come to a saving knowledge of God. Perhaps they had. Yet God required their lives when they thought they could lie to him with impunity. The lesson was not lost on the rest of the Christian community. The church was strengthened by their deaths, for "great fear came upon all the church, and upon as many as heard these things" (Acts 5:11). Sanctification begins with a healthy sense of awe for the God in whose presence we serve.

God hasn't struck anyone dead in your church lately? That may have been what the Corinthian Christians thought as well, but I believe Paul described physical sickness and death that had befallen abusers of the worship sacrament of the Lord's Supper: "For he that eateth and drinketh unworthily, eateth and drinketh damnation to himself, not discerning the Lord's body. For this cause many are weak and sickly among you, and many sleep" (1 Corinthians 11:29–30). Certainly the God who struck down Ananias and Sapphira hasn't changed his opinion of sin in his body, and he is one who should be regarded "acceptably with reverence and godly fear: For our God is a consuming fire" (Hebrews 12:28–29).

A more positive reason to be holy is that the transforming life should hunger for fellowship connection with the Beloved. If we were created to glorify God and enjoy him forever, the path of maturing holiness is the only way to achieve our most transforming purpose. Jesus came so that we may have life to the full (John 10:10). Why should we let anything keep us from enjoying all that life can be in Jesus?

Another reason for concern may seem obvious, but many overlook it: If we love God we should be willing and anxious to obey him. "If ye love me, keep my commandments," Jesus said in John 14:15, 23. Holiness is commanded.

Can I lose my salvation?

A child of God, bought with the blood of Christ, will not lose the salvation Jesus purchased. Not ever. Not under any circumstances. Theologians call this promise the doctrine of *eternal security* or the *perseverance of the saints*. According to Psalm 37:23–24, "The steps of a good man are ordered by the LORD: and he delighteth in his way. Though he fall, he shall not be utterly cast down: for the LORD upholdeth him with his hand."

This must have been a particularly important promise to John, for his Gospel quoted several of Jesus' statements regarding this assurance of life:

Verily, verily, I say unto you, He that heareth my word, and believeth on him that sent me, hath everlasting life, and shall not come into condemnation; but is passed from death unto life. [5:24]

All that the Father giveth me shall come to me; and him that cometh to me I will in no wise cast out. And this is the Father's will which hath sent me, that of all which he hath given me I should lose nothing, but should raise it up again at the last day. And this is the will of him that sent me that every one which seeth the Son, and believeth on him, may have everlasting life: and I will raise him up at the last day. [6:37, 39–40]

My sheep hear my voice, and I know them, and they follow me: And I give unto them eternal life; and they shall never perish, neither shall any man pluck them out of my hand. My Father, which gave them me, is greater than all; and no man is able to pluck them out of my Father's hand. I and my Father are one. [10:27–30]

My salvation is as certain as the promise of God and the oneness of the Father and the Son (see also Romans 8:29, 38–39).

But as clear as this promise stands, those who teach that one can lose salvation have a point: The one who claims Christ, yet shows no turning from sin or growth in Christian maturity and righteousness that naturally accompanies sanctification, has no ground for assurance of salvation. Such people have not *lost* salvation; they have not had it to lose. Jesus told a parable of a sower who scattered seed throughout his field (Matthew 13). One of the soils where seed landed was mostly rocks. At first the seed showed every appearance of sprouting but there was nothing for it to take root in, so the plant quickly withered in time of trouble (Luke 8:13).

Likewise seed fell among weeds. Again, it showed some signs of germination, but the weeds never moved over to allow room for a plant. This, Jesus said, represented the souls in which God's Word is choked out by worldly care. How many people seem to come to Christ (perhaps again and again), but their approach seems all emotion, with no change of direction or mind? They are not in love with Christ, nor do they make him Lord of their life. They wish an emotional high, a feel-good glow. Be cautious of such cathartic experiences. They are easy for Satan to mimic, and they often have little or nothing to do with the content of God's Word. At the first descent into the valley of life cares the person falls away. Others believe all of the right things, but their faith is so filled with shallow pride that love for God finds no place to take root. Such people may be filled with self-righteousness and very Bible literate, but they are bound for hell and never notice their plight.

In its chapter on the assurance of grace and salvation (18) the *Westminster Confession* speaks of times when assurance is lost:

> When one who has confessed Christ does not persevere in faith and commitment
> When one falls into a sin that wounds the conscience and grieves God's Spirit
> During times of severe temptation
> When one perceives that God has withdrawn—usually because we have withdrawn ourselves emotionally from God's presence or are in depression

There are indeed times when we need to look at our lives honestly and confess: I don't feel connected to God. Am I living in rebellion or forsaking his gifts of Scripture, prayer, and worship? If so, maybe I have not truly accepted him as Lord and need to approach God in repentance and submission.

We must be clear about the difference between believing intellectually or emotionally, but without submission. That is not faith. Evil spirits fell down before Jesus with the confession, "Thou art the Son of God" (Mark 3:11), but Jesus did not say, "Bless you, demon. You have finally seen the light." He told the devils to shut up, for he would accept no such belief or confession. The neighbors of the Gadarene demoniacs believed Jesus had power. But they wanted none of it

(Matthew 8:33–34). The people of Nazareth heard Jesus and were amazed at his wisdom and miracles, yet he condemned their faithlessness (Matthew 13:56–58). Many in Jerusalem saw his miracles and "believed in his name," records John 2:23, "But Jesus did not commit himself unto them, because he knew all men, And needed not that any should testify of man: for he knew what was in man" (2:24–25). Paul (Ephesians 2:8–10) and James (James 2:18–26) distinguish intellectual assent, which we share with demons (James 2:19), from saving faith that flows into sanctification. Works of obedience, righteousness, growth, and repentance do not save, but they are prerequisite to assurance of true redemption in Christ.

What do I have to do in sanctification?

Sanctification is a work of God in me, yet Christians are continually called to obedience as part of the working out of salvation. This sounds confusing, but it isn't so difficult to understand. Any large construction project is the work of more than one contractor, and God is pleased to subcontract part of this mammoth undertaking to the Christian. Or think of it as a partnership in which God provides the strength and will with which I keep my end of the contract. It is a good thing we have such assistance, for the goals of sanctification are perfection, identification with God, conformity to Christ, and a life of good works.

Through the process of sanctification the Christian joins in the work of God and others. As already stated, the Christian's perfection is an accomplished work of the Father, who sees us as perfect in Christ (1 Thessalonians 5:23). It also is a work of the Son. Jesus offered complete sanctification to the Father, fulfilling all righteousness (Matthew 3:15). The author of Hebrews says that Christ's obedience through suffering was a perfection that enabled him to be the perfect High Priest who offered himself as a perfect Sacrifice to be the Source of our salvation (Colossians 1:22; Hebrews 5:9–10). Jesus said in his prayer to the Father on the night before he was crucified: "For their sakes I sanctify myself, that they also might be sanctified through the truth" (John 17:19). And sanctification continues through God the Holy Spirit. "To the end he may stablish your hearts unblameable in holiness before God, even our Father, at the coming of our Lord Jesus Christ with all his saints" (1 Thessalonians 3:13).

The completion of sanctification in the individual extends beyond God to the work of the church, which prays for and enfolds the developing saint. Each member of the body strengthens the others and is strengthened in the Word by the others: "We are glad, when we are weak, and ye are strong: and this also we wish, even your perfection" (2 Corinthians 13:9; see also Colossians 1:28; 2 Timothy 3:16).

Perfection in sanctification holiness is aided, too, by circumstances—especially those we might prefer not to have. But as we work through them with growing dependence on God, we are working through our construction in holiness: "My brethren, count it all joy when ye fall into divers temptations; Knowing this, that the trying of our faith worketh patience. But let patience have her perfect work, that ye may be perfect and entire, wanting nothing" (James 1:2–4). In this we are actively involved: "Do all things without murmurings and disputings: That ye may be blameless and harmless, the sons of God, without rebuke, in the midst of a crooked and perverse nation, among whom ye shine as lights in the world" (Philippians 2:14–15; see also 2 Peter 3:14; 1 John 4:12).

*In sanctification's growing holiness the believer iden-
tifies with the perfection of God.* Identification with
the Father is what Jesus calls for when he says, "Be ye
therefore perfect, even as your Father which is in
heaven is perfect" (Matthew 5:48). Though God makes
us holy, the Christian is commanded to take off the old
attitudes and desires and to put on a new self, "which
after God is created in righteousness and true holiness"
(Ephesians 4:24). God is working behind the scenes on
such a reconstruction job, but he wants us to pound in
some nails. Ephesians 5:1–2a tells us to "Be ye therefore followers of God as dear children: And walk in
love, as Christ also hath loved us." Adds Paul elsewhere
in Ephesians, God has chosen us "that we should be
holy and without blame before him in love" (Ephesians
1:4b). Children imitate the father they love, and
shouldn't we be merciful, just as our Father is merciful (Luke 6:36)? Shouldn't we be kind one to another,
tenderhearted, forgiving one another, even as God for
Christ's sake forgave us (Ephesians 4:32)? Following in
Father's footsteps here is working alongside of him for
my sanctification. My work so fits into God's that I cannot say where my effort fades into his.

*Conformity to Christ means that sanctification
makes us think and act more like him.* Again, we know
that this conformity isn't anything we do (see pp.
99–101). In a real sense every Christian is conformed
to Christ the moment Christ's Holy Spirit dwells within.
The Christian has the mind of Christ (1 Corinthians
2:16) and increasingly reflects Christ's glory (2 Corinthians 3:18). But look at who all is at work in Ephesians
4:11–13, conforming us to Christ:

> And he gave some, apostles; and some, prophets; and
> some, evangelists; and some, pastors and teachers; For
> the perfecting of the saints, for the work of the min-

istry, for the edifying of the body of Christ: Till we all come in the unity of the faith, and of the knowledge of the Son of God, unto a perfect man, unto the measure of the stature of the fulness of Christ.

Our lives, as we become sanctified, should be reflected in works in keeping with who we are. What we do certainly reflects on the One we name as our master: "No man can serve two masters: for either he will hate the one, and love the other; or else he will hold to the one, and despise the other. Ye cannot serve God and mammon" (Matthew 6:24). "Let your light so shine before men, that they may see your good works, and glorify your Father which is in heaven" (Matthew 5:16). Peter tells us to be sanctified before the watching world: "Having your conversation honest among the Gentiles: that, whereas they speak against you as evil-doers, they may by your good works, which they shall behold, glorify God in the day of visitation" (1 Peter 2:12). James is caustic on this point:

> What doth it profit, my brethren, though a man say he hath faith, and have not works? can faith save him? If a brother or sister be naked, and destitute of daily food, And one of you say unto them, Depart in peace, be ye warmed and filled; notwithstanding ye give them not those things which are needful to the body; what doth it profit? Even so faith, if it hath not works, is dead, being alone. [2:14–17]

Even here we do not work alone. Paul says to be filled with the fruit of righteousness "which are by Jesus Christ, unto the glory and praise of God" (Philippians 1:11b). Ephesians 2:10 fits the partnership together: "For we are his workmanship, created in Christ Jesus unto good works, which God hath before ordained that we should walk in them."

Knowing the holiness of God

Having been justified, we are removed from our liability to punishment. Clothed with the garments of Christ, we stand judicially pure before God. In that context we are commanded to put sanctification into operation, to become pure on the inside so as not to dishonor those garments of grace. This is the matter to which sanctification addresses itself: "For I am the LORD your God: ye shall therefore sanctify yourselves, and ye shall be holy; for I am holy" (Leviticus 11:44a). Without holiness no one shall see God (Hebrews 12:14).

We are to perfect holiness in the fear of the Lord. If there is any one thing the church needs today it is a view of the holiness and majesty of God and a consequent view of his demand upon us. John calls us to look honestly on the worldliness that continues to corrupt our lives.

> If any man love the world, the love of the Father is not in him. For all that is in the world, the lust of the flesh, and the lust of the eyes, and the pride of life, is not of the Father, but of the world. And the world passeth away, and the lust thereof: but he that doeth the will of God abideth forever. [1 John 2:15b–17]

What is your particular form of corruption? Does it steal into your heart as a craving of the flesh? God calls us to holiness in body, mind, and spirit. Replace rottenness with that which is sound and holy. How many minds today are virtually pornographic? How about the body, which God commands to be presented as a living sacrifice, holy and acceptable and unconformed to the pattern of the world (Romans 12:1–2)? Is it holy or contaminated by vile deeds and habits? Is your spirit holy? What about the lust of the eyes (covetousness)? The Bible says covetousness is corruption in his sight (Matthew 5:28). What about boasting pride in what you have or do? Vain ambition, pride in appearance, pride in knowledge, pride in ability? These are forms of vile rottenness, out of conformity to Christ who says, "Take my yoke upon you, and learn of me; for I am meek and lowly in heart: and ye shall find rest unto your souls" (Matthew 11:29).

We are called to use the means of sanctification—the Word of God, prayer, obedience to God's commands, the sacraments, and worship together with a family of believers. The Holy Spirit takes our use of these means and makes them the method by which he sanctifies us. If you would know God's holiness, then use the means he has given you to know it.

1. Spend time in prayer.
2. Seriously, systematically meditate upon the Word of God.
3. Walk in a more determined obedience. Many a Christian is determined to walk in *most* of the ways of God's commandments, yet gets nowhere because of the unexplored areas that seem too much trouble. Repentance requires determination after total new obedience.

Would you know the holiness of God? Then you will have to know him who is holy, for apart from him, the thrice-holy God, nothing inhabits this sin-tainted world but death and corruption. Draw near to him. Show the glint of gold—the fruitful holiness of sanctification.

What is saving faith?

The grace of faith, whereby the elect are enabled to believe to the saving of their souls, is the work of the Spirit of Christ in their hearts, and is ordinarily wrought by the ministry of the Word; by which also, and by the administration of the sacraments and prayer it is increased and strengthened.
[Westminster Confession of Faith, chapter 14]

6

Three-Dimensional Faith

t was a dark night on the Mississippi highway from Jackson to Vicksburg. The sky was overcast, but at least the heavy rains of the last few days had stopped. The truck driver relaxed in the cab of his truck and watched the broken line of the road disappear monotonously beneath his cab, thankful that at least now the roads were dry and much safer.

Suddenly the twin taillights on the car in front of him melted into the road and disappeared! He sat bolt upright in his cab. That was inexplicable. It could not happen, and yet it just had. That thought went through his mind in a fraction of a second. In the next fraction of a second he saw the gaping black hole where a bridge had stood over the river.

He slammed on the brakes. The wheels stopped instantly, but there was no longer any road beneath them. His truck sailed silently and eerily into the black void. Breaking glass, he extricated himself and managed to swim to shore. He scrambled up the embankment, all the while hearing one car after another zoom smoothly into the gap, and disappear, followed by shrieks and a booming splash.

Finally he reached the road and frantically waved his hands at oncoming cars. They were no doubt surprised by this dripping scarecrow, but at least three passed him by before he was able to stop a driver from speeding over the edge. Sixteen people died that night. Each had faith in a bridge that the swollen river had torn away—a bridge that was out.

Many suppose that by the bridge of good works—morality, piety, church membership, good character, and religiosity—they can somehow make their way across that dark river safely into paradise. That bridge is out. The abyss is real, and it is eternal. I cannot imagine how frightening it must be to feel yourself, at the end of life, silently slipping over the edge into eternity without heeding God's call—without being justified, adopted, and sanctified.

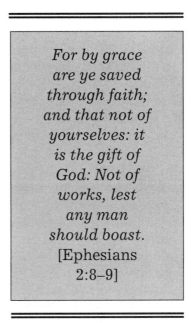

For by grace are ye saved through faith; and that not of yourselves: it is the gift of God: Not of works, lest any man should boast. [Ephesians 2:8–9]

We have seen what is required of God for salvation to become a reality. In chapters 6 and 7 we will see two things that are required of us: saving faith and repentance. Actually we have already looked at the first of these. Faith is step five in the outline of a plan of salvation that was presented in the introduction to book 2. Here is the bridge that crosses the river safely:

5. Faith
   a. What it is not: intellectual assent or temporal faith
   b. What it is: trusting in Jesus Christ alone

Saving, sanctifying faith is a work of God in our lives, but a mysterious work of God in which we play an active part. Growing in that faith is the transforming enterprise of sanctification, as we grow in seeking to glorify God and to enjoy him forever. It is the one most important ingredient in a life lived for God—a life worth living, and a life that stretches beyond the shadows of earth.

Unraveling the mystery

The *Westminster Confession of Faith* defines saving faith as "the work of the Spirit of Christ" that enables the elect to believe. Once again, the belief in view is no intellectual assent, nor is it emotion, though the Holy Spirit works both in the mind and the emotions to produce it. Saving faith is a reordering of mind, emotions, and will around a central proposition that we are absolutely certain is true. The *Confession*'s chapter on saving faith carefully describes what this means in daily life terms:

> By this faith a Christian believeth to be true whatsoever is revealed in the Word, for the authority of God himself speaking therein; and acteth differently upon that which each particular passage thereof containeth; yielding obedience to the commands, trembling at the threatenings, and embracing the promises of God for this life and that which is to come. But the principle acts of saving faith are accepting, receiving, and resting upon Christ alone for justification, sanctification, and eternal life, by virtue of the covenant of grace.

Notice that the Christian does not work to *find* this faith. He or she *has* it. But *by this faith* Christianity becomes a living force in the individual and in the individual's world. *Faith* is the ultimate action word of Christianity. Grammatically it may be a noun, but in our sanctification faith acts as the empowering verb.

A mind in submission to truth

By this faith the Christian *believes to be true whatsoever is revealed in the Word*. This does not mean the rational mind jumps over a mystical precipice. Quite the opposite. The rational mind is confident in the truth of the Scriptures because the authority of God is known to stand behind them. When a proposition comes along that seems to refute some truth in God's Word, saving faith is grounded in a firm base of authority and so is not blown away with the first cannonade volley. Rather the intellect, in submission to the Scriptures, kicks into a higher gear to investigate, knowing that all is not as it appears:

1. Is this new fact as factual as it appears, or is someone blowing smoke to make it look like unshakeable truth?
2. What is the logic of these facts? Have they been arranged in such a way as to bias the results? (This is a particularly important question in thinking through claims made in the sciences where researchers unintentionally color their findings according to what they "know" to be true. Recall book 1's example of the pre-human tooth that actually came from the mouth of a pig.)
3. Similarly, what are the presuppositions of those who have come up with this new "truth"? Do they have a hidden agenda?

4. What, precisely, does Scripture say about this subject? Have I been reading more into the text than is actually there, or misinterpreting something as literal that was written as figurative?

Many dates have been set for the Lord's return and the end of the world, using a creative reading of Scriptures. When the key date passed, some fell away from faith, when they should have fallen away from their naïve Bible teachers. Saving faith disciplines the mind under God's authority, correctly interpreting Scripture and carefully evaluating teachings in the light of solid personal study. We should heed Paul's advice to Timothy to be "a workman that needeth not to be ashamed, rightly dividing the word of truth" (2 Timothy 2:15).

When thoughtful, disciplined submission to the Word is practiced, faith is strengthened, rather than destroyed, by attacks on the authenticity of the Word. The Christian builds a healthy skepticism about human experts and the latest "revelation from God" received by some supposed evangelist.

One rather humorous case in point occurred recently in a gathering of New Testament scholars who decided that they were going to settle once and for all what Jesus did and did not say among his words quoted in the Gospels. The media evidently found this symposium particularly significant, for most newspapers and magazines disseminated the experts' astute findings to an extent unusual for an academic convocation. I don't know how many people really took these proceedings seriously, but the scholars took themselves seriously. That made their report all the more amusing. They divided all the quoted sayings of Christ into two categories: (1) his teachings on social justice and (2) everything else he is reported to have said, such as his uncomfortable moral commands or statements that he was God and the only way to salvation. Can you guess which statements were found to be genuine? At the feet of these scholars we learn for certain that Jesus wasn't God, but at least he was politically correct. Many attacks on Christianity are not quite so ridiculous, but most can be seen for what they are under critical examination with the mind of faith, the mind submitted to Scripture.

A life in submission to truth

By faith a Christian is prepared to change his thinking and his actions on the basis of what Scripture says. This faith also is based upon the certain knowledge that the very authority of God stands behind what is taught in his Word. Saving faith is ready to act upon what Scripture says. According to the *Confession*, the man or woman of faith reads Scripture diligently and attends to the preaching of the Word. The mind works critically in this regard. Using the example of setting a date for the return of Christ, suppose you are listening to a preacher who has discovered a hidden message in the number of letters contained in the King James text of Daniel 12. With some additional help from Matthew 24 and the number of words printed in red in his copy of Revelation, this teacher proclaims that the tribulation will strike next year, probably in February, and that you are called upon to sell all of your belongings and come gather to await the return of the Lord seven years hence.

A life in submission to the authority of God would not rush right home from hearing this dire message and hold a garage sale, selling even the garage. The mind disciplined by saving faith would have to be satisfied first about what Scripture really says and so asks more questions:

1. Does this interpretation of Scripture go along with clear passages through the rest of the Bible (for example, about not knowing the day or the hour at which the Master will come)?
2. Is this interpretation based upon clearly revealed teachings of what the text actually says? If this interpretation differs from what the church historically has taught in this regard, are there solid grounds for believing this particular Bible scholar has found something that has been missed by most others (which is seldom the case)?
3. Is the teacher basing all that is said on the authority of God or upon his or her own "new light"? If the teacher claims some new revelation of truth, the answer is obvious—that claim must be rejected on the basis of Hebrews 1:1. All revelation is now from Christ, and Christ has revealed himself in Scripture. There are new applications as the Holy Spirit relates the never-changing words of God to the changing context of our lives, but no new precepts.

You have the practice of reading your horoscope column each morning and ordering your life according to what an astrologer sees in the stars. Then you come to Christ, are regenerated, and begin to seek to follow God's will through faith. At first, as a new believer with a lot of old ways of living, you may not make a connection between reading the horoscope column and trusting the God who rules the heavens and the earth. You might even decide that God put the stars where they are, so that is why they influence our lives. Then one day a neighbor takes you aside and lovingly points out that the Bible has strong words to say against astrology and that the Christian is to leave behind those elements of the world and conform to a new pattern of faith. A choice must be made: Will you submit to God's revealed authority and repent of what he condemns?

The person with saving faith may have problems getting rid of the old habits, but he or she has no question about who has the authority and must be obeyed.

What if the application to life is not so clear-cut? A teacher says you must live one way because that is what the Bible says. You read those passages yourself, and you aren't so certain that this is a correct interpretation. Or another teacher contends that the text says something entirely different. Such questions must be answered carefully, with much prayer for discernment and the help of others more mature in faith. When a text is unclear and seems open to more than one view, there is a more certain text elsewhere that covers at least the principle behind the question. God sometimes makes us dig for the truth, but he never leaves important truth unavailable. However the search for truth proceeds, if the heart is intent on obeying what Scripture actually says, faith will be nurtured toward maturity (James 1:2–5). The key principles of saving faith involve where the individual looks for ultimate authority and whether the individual is willing to submit to that authority.

Mind and life in submission to Christ

Submission to the authority of Scripture obviously has much to do with God's working of saving faith in the believer's life. However, the *Confession* goes on to relate that this is a subordinate part of the story. "But the principle acts of saving faith are accepting, receiving, and resting upon Christ alone for justification, sanctification, and eternal life, by virtue of the covenant of grace." Faith is at its most active when pointed at Christ as Lord of the covenant of grace. We *do* faith through three dimensions:

1. accepting
2. receiving
3. resting

Those may not sound like very active words, but in God's economy they act within the mystery of the dual source of faith—God and the believer. Saving faith has its source in us as we live accepting, receiving, resting lives of submission to Christ and his truth. And the source of saving faith is in God. It is his Holy Spirit that accepts, receives, and rests through us. But where does our part leave off and God's begin? When does intellectual assent to the truth, which does not save, become righteousness-dispensing grace that does?

Living faith in three dimensions

Accept, receive, and *rest* are three separate, repetitive actions of the sanctifying Christian life. They begin in a once-for-all act. The lost, hopeless unbeliever is confronted with the claims of Christ and sees in them the only hope for peace with God. Christ extends the good news, asking, "Will you accept me into your life as Savior and Lord?" The Holy Spirit enables the words of this message to sink into the consciousness and a life of rebellion to be turned to faith that this message is true and available. The response: "Yes! Yes, I believe, that Jesus is the Christ, God become human of a virgin, who died to take the penalty for my sins and conquered death so that I may never die. Yes, I cast myself on you."

In that moment of *accepting*, the Holy Spirit already is working another sort of faith in the one who is being reborn. The truth and lordship of Christ have been accepted mentally and emotionally; now the cleansing, justifying, adopting work of Christ is *received* and the faith worked in the person by the Holy Spirit is accounted by the Father as righteousness in the sacrifice of Christ. At the same time a third dimension of spirituality is born into the soul: a new worldview or organizing principle that revolutionizes the reborn life. The person's life foundation had been built upon external morality and selfishness, but now the basis for making choices and relating to self, others, and God *rests* upon submissive, obedient, saving faith:

1. The reborn Christian *accepts* the gospel as a personal reality.
2. The reborn Christian *receives* Christ's righteousness before God.
3. The reborn Christian *rests* his or her life on a new foundation.

All three are God's works and our acceptance of Christ in faith comes through the Holy Spirit. It is "not of works, lest any man should boast" (Ephesians 2:9). The founder of Gordon College and a missions leader of the nineteenth century, A. J. Gordon, once was riding on a train when he presented the gospel to the man seated next to him. He had explained that it is through faith in Christ that we are redeemed, when the man broke in, "Sir, I heartily disagree with you. I do not believe for one instant that God is going to admit a man to heaven merely on the basis of some little scrap of theological paper which you call faith. But, rather, I believe that God will make a searching inquiry into one's character and morals and his good works." As he said this the conductor came by, and they offered him their tickets.

"Did you notice," asked Gordon a moment later, "how that conductor eyed our tickets very carefully and paid virtually no attention to our persons or our character?"

Even the dimension of receiving, which would seem utterly passive, has an active element. I have known people who refuse to take the action of receiving righteousness. They may, in fact, be saved children of God, but they seemingly have never mentally received as theirs the assurance of forgiveness promised by Scripture. For whatever reason in the past or present, such people live as if unforgiven and fret that the joy and victory that other believers experience have not come. There is no victory of faith, for the sin of self-unforgiveness affronts the God who has forgiven. Failure to receive God's promises is a self-induced birth defect in faith that nurses a grudge and denies that God can keep those promises. It might be that faith has never been born, but possibly it means the person rebelliously gets perverse, childish satisfaction in self-punishment.

Faith is recumbency

Three-dimensional faith does not just work at the moment of salvation. The process works over and over, every day of the born-again life. Living, saving faith is not *just* the bridge over the river we will someday cross. If that is all it is in one's thinking, saving faith is not yet part of the life. Nor is saving faith a toll booth we pass to get to God's super highway. Saving faith is both the bridge at the end of earthly life and the highway beneath the wheels. Through that faith the Christian "believes to be true whatsoever is revealed in the Word" for today, whether faith that God can help overcome some illness, face the challenge of service, or deal with a problem with sin. Through three-dimensional faith God enables his child to

1. *accept* what the Bible says as a personal reality,
2. *receive* the promises that pertain to God's presence and direction in that kind of situation, and
3. move out with assurance that *rests* on the foundation of Christ.

The Puritans of the seventeenth and eighteenth centuries used an interesting term to describe this faith. Saving faith, said the Puritans, is *recumbency*. Missionary John Paton grasped the meaning of that word when he began to translate the Gospel of John for the natives of the New Hebrides. He discovered that their language seemed to contain no word for *faith*. Yet the gospel would hardly make sense without it. After weeks of mulling over this linguistic puzzle, he returned to his home after a long journey with his guide. His native friend sat in a chair on the porch, put his feet up on a stool, heaved a great sigh of relief, and said something Paton could not understand. After some explanation Paton finally understood that the single word his native guide used meant, "I have rested all of my weight here."

That was it! That was what the Puritans had meant by *recumbency* or recumbent faith. Saving faith rests all the weight upon the Lord.

Charles Spurgeon had a similar illustration for recumbent faith. A limpet is a small mollusk with a cone-shaped shell that lives by the seashore. It does one thing outstandingly: It has a foot by which it clings tenaciously to a rock or the underneath side of a ship. Spurgeon said that if you sneak up quietly on a limpet and hit it with a stick it will fall off the rock. But then try to hit another limpet nearby. It has been warned. You can hit it until you break your stick, but you will not knock it from the rock. It will hold on as if it knows its very life depends on clinging to the rock. "Faith," said Spurgeon, "is clinging to Jesus Christ." In the midst of the tumultuous seas of this world it is clinging to Christ as if salvation itself depends on him. Faith is the key to heaven, but it is not just knowing about Jesus Christ. Nor is it trusting God for such things as safety, health, and wealth, which are temporal and will pass away. Saving faith is clinging to Jesus Christ alone for salvation. Only as we depend totally on him can we know that God has forgiven us and made us new. "Believe on the Lord Jesus Christ, and thou shalt be saved" (Acts 16:31).

This is faith that behaves differently and thinks differently because it is focused on Jesus Christ and his work to bring the Christian through justification, sanctification, and eternal life into a covenant relationship with God. The Christian's presuppositions about the world differ from those of others because of the working of scriptural truth into the mind—the foundation. Saving faith cannot help but make substantive changes in all that a person is. That is the distinction James makes between faith and works (James 1:22–27; 2:14–25). There is a kind of faith that is intellect or all emotion—all bells and whistles, flash and mirrors—but no substance. That is the sort the Bible calls "dead." To understand the dimensions of alive faith we begin with Ephesians 2:8–9. By God's grace we are saved *through faith*. Here is the first clue to the mystery.

Faith is the conduit

Through faith means "by" or "by means of faith."
Yet we can speak of *through* in another sense as well,
for faith acts as a conduit. Through it courses the grace
of God. In the Holy Land I remember visiting a massive Roman aqueduct along the eastern shore of the
Mediterranean. It stretched as far as the eye could see.
This aqueduct was perhaps fifteen or twenty feet high
and massive, supported by thousands of arches. The
centuries have not been kind to this wonder, and for
many centuries it has lain unused. There were great
gaps in the aqueduct, and it no longer carried water to
the Roman capital. That is what our faith is like. It is
the aqueduct that brings to us the water of grace. The
water of grace is the important thing, but grace moves
through an intact aqueduct of faith.

An elderly woman was known to have led a serene,
victorious life. People were curious to know the secret
through which she had been so blessed and had blessed
others. One person looked her up and asked, "Are you
the woman with the great faith?" She responded, "No,
but I am a woman with a great God." She had learned
that it is not the conduit that helps us; it is the water
that flows through it. In the great cities of the Roman
world aqueducts channeled water to fountains where
the people drew water in pots for their families. The
Romans enjoyed giving things an aesthetic appeal, and
they developed fantastically carved stone and bronze
statuary to decorate their fountains. The life of faith
is attractive. God crafted the faith of this woman into
something lovely to behold, something whose very
beauty pointed others to Christ. The important thing
of the aqueducts and fountains, however, was the
water, and the importance of faith is the grace it car-
ries. That is what the writers of the *Westminster Con-*

fession realized when they said of saving faith, the conduit of grace:

> This faith is different in degrees, weak or strong; may
> be often and many ways assailed and weakened, but
> gets the victory; growing up in many to the attainment
> of a full assurance through Christ, who is both the
> author and finisher of our faith.

Nurturing three-dimensional faith

Time, conquerors, and the elements ravaged those
strong Roman conduits. Throughout the New Testament
Christians are being urged to keep in good repair and
strengthen their faith, so that it can quench the flaming
arrows of Satan in the day of battle (Ephesians 6:16).
The *Confession*, then, gives some good advice to those
who feel weak and uncertain. This advice begins in the
observation that saving faith usually comes into an
unbeliever as the Holy Spirit applies Scripture. God
normally chooses to bring saving faith through the
ministry of the Word. It may come as a preacher applies
a Bible passage, or as a seeker remembers some long-
ago Sunday school lesson or opens the Bible to seek
answers. It may come through the witness of a believer
who shares the good news. The point is that the Holy
Spirit applies the content of Scripture in the context of
the sinner's experience.

If that is how one comes to have saving faith, faith
for living also is strengthened through the same com-
bination of Scripture and experience: "the ministry of
the Word, the administration of the sacraments, and
prayer." One comes to experience a recumbent faith as
one experiences God. The longer and more fully the

conduit has been carrying water, the more natural comes the trust of God as Friend. The friend of God is blessed whose delight is in the law of the Lord, attached to the conduit of grace, "and he shall be like a tree planted by the rivers of water, that bringeth forth his fruit in his season; his leaf also shall not wither; and whatsoever he doeth shall prosper" (Psalm 1:3).

Scripture sets before us a model for what living, three-dimensional faith should look like. If the life of faith can be seen as an Olympic event Abraham is scored as the record holder. A close look at that record-shattering event, however, tells us a lot about how faith is nurtured. Abraham's life shows the attainable faith that fails more often than it succeeds, but in the end still stands. Abraham's faith faltered more often than it conquered, and it matured over many years.

God's call on Abram in Ur of the Chaldees was unexpected and possibly unwanted. Ur was the foremost city of the world, and Abram was a well-connected Ur urbanite whose family had likely bowed for generations to the moon god, the chief deity of the Chaldeans. God called on Abram to leave behind the settled lands of Ur and Haran and make a career move at age seventy-five—to become a wandering patriarch. He was to leave behind all but his own immediate family and strike out alone. He was to leave behind allegiance to old relationships and former gods to follow the God who would make of him a nation, at best a long-term project. Abram accepted the call and immediately obeyed all of God's direction in faith, right? Not quite.

Abram took along much of his family, including Lot, whose lifestyle and godliness were anything but exemplary. At the first sign of famine, Abram left the land to which God had sent him for the safety of Egypt. While in Egypt he passed off his wife Sarai as his sister in an act of cowardice. He only returned to where he was supposed to be when he was deported. When God wasn't quick enough to give him a son he tried to help God out, first by offering his servant to be his heir and then fathering a child by a servant girl. When God told him that the promise would not come through this son Ishmael, but through a son yet to be born, he argued to try to place the blessing on Ishmael instead. And to show that he was, indeed, a slow learner he then became afraid of another king and tried to pass off his wife as his sister once again.

Throughout these years the Bible also records how Abram, whose name became *Abraham*, called upon God and slowly learned more about God's covenant promise with him and God's great provision for him. Ever so slowly his faith was taking three-dimensional form. But the final test of that mature faith came perhaps fifty years after Abram received that first call of God. His son Isaac was born when he was 100 years old, and he saw that child of promise grow into adulthood.

Only then did God give Abraham his final challenge, one that thrills and horrifies us in Genesis 22: "Take now thy son, thine only son Isaac, whom thou lovest, and get thee into the land of Moriah; and offer him there for a burnt offering upon one of the mountains which I will tell thee of" (v. 2). It sounds a monstrous thing for God to suggest, but oddly we are not told that Abraham presented any of his usual arguments. He simply got up, cut the wood, gathered Isaac and his servants, and set out.

When Mount Moriah was visible in the distance, Abraham and Isaac left their servants with a singular confidence about what was to come: "Abide ye here with the ass; and I and the lad will go yonder and worship, *and come again to you*" (v. 5). Isaac turns to his father, remarking that they have not brought the lamb of sacrifice. His father answers, "My son, God will provide himself a lamb for a burnt offering" (v. 8). Yet God does not provide until the altar is built, the wood is placed, Isaac is bound and placed on the altar, and the knife is raised to strike. Only in that last second did an angel intervene with the ram that was to replace the son.

Living faith took the chance that God was faithful, based on the faithfulness God had shown in the past, based on the Word of God, based on long conversations and even arguments with God in prayer, based on past personal failures through which God had been faithful.

Not yet ready to sacrifice a son on the altar for God? Through faith we realize that in Jesus that will not be necessary. For we know what Abraham could only dimly see, that Mount Moriah would, many hundreds of years later, be the site of a city called Jerusalem, where God would place his Son, his only Son Jesus, whom he loved, on the altar for us.

Only he did not stay his hand. Such love is strong enough that we can take recumbency in it. And when we realize that through growing faith, then we are ready for our own walk up Moriah.

What does it mean to repent?

Repentance unto life is an evangelical grace. . . . By it a sinner, out of the sight and sense, not only of the danger, but also of the filthiness and odiousness of his sins, as contrary to the holy nature and righteous law of God, and upon the apprehension of his mercy in Christ to such as are penitent, so grieves for and hates his sins as to turn from them all unto God, purposing and endeavoring to walk with him in all the ways of his commandments. [Westminster Confession of Faith, chapter 15]

7

The Gift of a Broken Heart

epentance and faith are inseparable in Scripture. There can be no genuine repentance without faith. There is no genuine faith without repentance. The two are heads and tails of one coin.

On the day the church was born, the day of Pentecost, pilgrims from all over the Jewish world were visiting Jerusalem. A multitude of them gathered to see the strange happenings outside one house that was perhaps not far from the temple. A group of men shouted to them in all of their own languages. The city was packed with people for the holy day, and dozens, then hundreds, then thousands strained to hear the story of Jesus of Nazareth. They heard that this teacher and healer was the very Son of God, the long-expected Messiah, that he had been killed by the religious leaders, and that God had raised him from death. Many had heard of this man, whose words and touch brought healing to the body and to the soul. Now they learned that he could make all things new. Thousands as one came to believe Peter's words that day. They knew that if all of this was true, then a response surely was demanded.

"Brothers, what shall we do?" they asked.

Peter did not launch into an explanation of justification by faith by the blood of Jesus Christ. Obviously, the Holy Spirit already was working faith into thousands of hearts. And with faith came understanding that it was their sins that had nailed God to a cross. The Bible says this thought pierced them emotionally as they had pierced the Christ physically. They were cut, wounded, and probed to the heart.

"What shall we do?"
"What is required of us?"
"What response is appropriate to such news?"

Peter told them to take the step that would seal their new allegiance to Christ—repent.

Faith and repentance

Repentance will not save. Yet you cannot be saved without it. Merely repenting of sin does not guarantee an entrance into heaven, any more than being sorry for committing murder

> *When they heard this, they were pricked in their heart, and said unto Peter and to the rest of the apostles, Men and brethren, what shall we do? Then Peter said unto them, Repent, and be baptized every one of you in the name of Jesus Christ for the remission of sins.* [Acts 2:37–38a]

guarantees that the prescribed penalty will not be exacted. Even repentance with true contrition, confession, and a promise not to do it again will not impress a judge and jury at a murder trial. It won't work with God either. A person also must give Jesus Christ a proper place as Lord of life.

Some people have a false faith that is merely intellectual assent. Counterfeit faith contains no tempered steel to cut to the heart. It accepts the facts, opines that they are interesting and even significant in a historical sort of way, and then turns to other matters. There is no crisis of understanding that this news demands personal attention, commitment, and an amended lifestyle. Some people have false repentance, deciding that what Christ requires is for them to try harder to keep the rules.

Counterfeit repentance decides that one can do enough to approach God. Counterfeit repentance of another sort endeavors to do better but trusts only in its own works.

True repentance in faith, by contrast, changes a person's perspective of God and the world, so that all things center in Jesus Christ. Through true repenting, faith changes God's perspective of the person, in that God no longer sees a rebel sinner, but rather a child whose sins are covered in the righteousness of Christ. True repentance changes a person by instilling God's perspective of the world and of life. Nothing so transforms a person's wants and wishes and loves as to see things from God's perspective. The *Westminster Confession* lists transforming elements that come with this new view of things:

1. The sinner sees and senses the danger of rebelling against God.

2. The sinner sees and senses how dirty and disgusting his or her sins appear to God.
3. The sinner sees and senses how holy and pure God is and what righteousness before God truly means in the light of Christ and the Word.
4. The sinner sees and senses that forgiving mercy has become available in Christ to the penitent.
5. The sinner grieves for and hates sins and turns from them all.
6. The sinner purposes and endeavors to walk with God in all the ways of his commandments.

The human soul is made up of mind, heart, and will, so all three are involved in these aspects of repentance. The person intellectually grasps that sin, because of its heinousness, will be punished, and that there is a divine remedy for sin. The sinner must come to know the way of salvation as it has been divinely appointed by God. Only through Christ, his grace, and death on the cross can eternal hope be found.

Legal strivings

Some of the deepest thinking on what it means to repent comes from an eighteenth-century pastor named Jonathan Edwards. The First Great Awakening in the 1730s turned a large portion of the population of New England back to God from a life of superficial faith and works righteousness. Edwards was one of the keenest tools of God in that revival. He is called by some the greatest theologian ever born on this continent. Observing how repentance and faith and how mind, heart, and will worked together in those he had seen turn to God, Edwards described a "legal striving" that first occurred when "the corruption of the heart first discovered itself." He observed how awakened understanding of God's holiness and personal sinfulness emotionally afflicted the soul:

> As they are gradually more and more convinced of the corruption and wickedness of their hearts, they seem to themselves to grow worse and worse, harder and blinder, and more desperately wicked, instead of growing better. They are ready to be discouraged by it, and oftentimes never think themselves so *far off* from good as when they are *nearest*. . . . When awakenings first begin, their consciences are commonly most exercised about their *outward* vicious course, or other acts of sin; but *afterwards* are more burdened with a sense of heart-sins, the dreadful corruption of their nature, their enmity against God, the pride of their hearts, their unbelief, their rejection of Christ, the Stubbornness and obstinacy of their wills; and the like. In many, God makes much use of their own experience, in the course of their awakenings and endeavors after saving good, to convince them of their own vile emptiness and universal depravity. [*A Narrative of Surprising Conversions,* section 2, italics in original]

Can such a discouraging view help the sinner find God and be part of faith and repentance? Edwards said that the deeper the sinner is drawn to probe the inner person and the more aware he or she understands this utter depravity, the greater the conviction of "absolute dependence on his sovereign power and grace." This feeling of absolute dependence transforms the heart of the sinner coming to God and the Christian who should be closer to God. It knocks out all the human props. The heart is broken as the mind understands the necessity of a Mediator. It hurts to contemplate personal wickedness and guilt, insufficiency and pollution, vile emptiness and lawlessness. But to the extent that I do understand those things I depend on God in faith, and my will is turned to wanting those things that benefit me and please God. Heart affections converge on God.

When Paul tells us in Ephesians 6:10–17 to put on the full armor of God so that we can stand against Satan, he starts with the belt of truth that is to be buckled around the waist. People in Paul's day knew that affections could take away appetite and give a flutter to the stomach, and so the seat of the emotions often was placed in the intestines, the belly and bowels. What could a greeting card company have done with that? There is no area of our being so prone to delusion as the emotions, so Paul tells us to clamp a solid belt of truth around them. No one comes to God or grows as a Christian without searching into the inner person, the dark corners that are often subconscious dwellings for dirty little creatures we didn't even know existed within us. To probe the self and repent of heart sins is a wrenching experience, but one King David knew was unavoidable if he were to find peace from the sin in his own life:

> Behold, I was shapen in iniquity and in sin did my mother conceive me. Behold thou desireth truth in the inward parts: and in the hidden part thou shalt make me to know wisdom. . . . Create in me a clean heart, O God; and renew a right spirit within me. . . . The sacrifices of God are a broken spirit: a broken and a contrite heart, O God, thou wilt not despise. [Psalm 51:5–6, 10, 17]

These legal strivings of the heart break the spirit as they show the cost of sin. In Old Testament times repentance for sin involved a demonstration of sin's offensiveness. The repentant worshiper purchased to sacrifice the best animal available—unblemished. Repentance came with cost. It involved cost for the one who brought the sacrifice and rather more cost for the animal whose throat was cut. A great many of those who came with their sacrifices to the altar were going through the motions of religious tradition, but those who got the point God was making saw that their sins inflicted hideous cost. That thought must have broken their heart as they contemplated the implications of the chasm between humanity and God. In Psalm 51 David saw that price, saying that a broken heart is the true sacrifice God wants. In Romans 12:1 Paul applies this brokenness to all of the life of faith. He urges us, "by the mercies of God, that ye present your bodies a living sacrifice, holy, acceptable unto God, which is your reasonable service." The broken and contrite believer continually brings the self and lays it on the altar in repentance and submission. A broken, contrite spirit is pliable, able to be bent and smoothed into the shape God desires, not the shape of the world pattern (Romans 12:2). Faith and repentance, resting in God and being broken to absolute dependence: This is the proper act of worship.

The lost doctrine of repentance

R. B. Kuiper wrote that people have lost sight of two things, and as a result, the church of the Lamb slain for sins no longer preaches that sinners must repent. First, they have lost the meaning of sin. It is seen as a trifle, a peccadillo, something that can be excused as part of being human. Even those set apart to lead seem to have forgotten that their nature is fallen, debased, depraved, and nothing like God first made it. They do not see that sin inevitably brings death. Second, people have lost the real vision of the holiness of God. They do not lift their eyes, so they never undergo the awakening described by Jonathan Edwards. They never abhor themselves and repent in dust and ashes.

Scripture stresses the importance of repentance. Both Old and New Testaments call upon people to repent. Noah was a preacher of righteousness, calling the doomed people around him to leave their wicked ways and turn to God. All the prophets called for a leaving of sin and a radical turning away to God. Ezekiel 18 proclaims one of the best explanations of how and why to repent:

> The soul that sinneth, it shall die. . . . But if the wicked will turn from all his sins that he hath committed, and keep all my statutes, and do that which is lawful and right, he shall surely live, he shall not die. Repent, and turn yourselves from all your transgressions; so iniquity shall not be your ruin. Cast away from you all your transgressions, whereby ye have transgressed; and make you a new heart and a new spirit: for why will ye die, O house of Israel? For I have no pleasure in the death of him that dieth, saith the Lord GOD: wherefore turn yourselves, and live ye. [vv. 20a, 21, 30b–32]

John the Baptist took up this refrain as a new day dawned over the world: "But when he saw many of the Pharisees and Sadducees come to his baptism, he said unto them, O generation of vipers, who hath warned you to flee from the wrath to come? Bring forth therefore fruits meet for repentance" (Matthew 3:7–8).

After Jesus reached his thirtieth year and began his ministry, Matthew records: "From that time Jesus began to preach, and to say, Repent: for the kingdom of heaven is at hand" (4:17). The burden of his heart and ministry for a world of sinners was that they should repent. One of his most beautiful parables concerned an errant, prodigal child who came to repentance (Luke 15:11–32). In nearby text he described the joy in heaven over a sinner who repents (v. 7). In Luke 13 disciples ask Jesus why "bad things happen to good people," to use the contemporary expression. They gave the example of an incident in which Galileans who came to the temple to worship were killed in a confrontation with Roman soldiers. What had these people done wrong to bring such judgment upon themselves in the very act of worship? "Suppose ye that these Galilaeans were sinners above all the Galilaeans, because they suffered such things? I tell you, Nay: but, except ye repent, ye shall all likewise perish" (vv. 2b–3).

Christians are to be about the proclamation of repentance. After Jesus' resurrection he told his disciples that repentance and forgiveness of sins was to be preached in the name of Jesus in all the world, for "ye are witnesses of these things" (Luke 24:47–48). The call to repentance was to be integral to gospel proclamation. At the end of Scripture this word still is on the lips of Jesus. Eight times in the Revelation of John he commands that his church should repent. In all, fifty-three times the New Testament commands men and women to repent.

One can't help but be struck by the theme of repentance when reading accounts of the awakenings in Edwards's Massachusetts, Asahel Nettleton's frontier West of the early 1800s, the Welsh revival in the early 1900s, or Korea's of the 1960s. There was an intensity of realized sin and absolute dependence on Jesus as Mediator. It was the seriousness with which Martin Luther appraised his own sin that gave justification by grace its revolutionizing power in the 1500s. Many church historians have tried to psychologize such workings in the heart, calling them products of an unhealthy society and self-image. But isn't it interesting that where deep repentance has oppressed, deep faith has flourished? Those who saw how much God had forgiven felt a debt of love.

Debtors to mercy

Indebtedness surely changes people. In Romans 1:14 this feeling of owed love empowers the apostle Paul: "I am debtor both to the Greeks, and to the Barbarians; both to the wise and to the unwise." What an enigmatic text. How could Paul have been a debtor to the Greeks and to the non-Greeks? What had they done for him? Let us look at some of the things they did for him:

> Five times he was beaten with thirty-nine lashes.
> Three times he was beaten with rods.
> Once he was stoned and left for dead.
> He was shipwrecked.
> He was in danger from Jews, in danger from Gentiles, in danger from robbers, without food, sleep, clothing.
> He carried around the burdens of hundreds of Christians around the known world (2 Corinthians 11:23–33).

Nevertheless, Paul felt a debt, a master motive that impelled a forceful life: Jesus Christ had given him everything. He could only give obedient love and faithfulness in return. Paul had life everlasting, forgiveness for the "chief of sinners," pardon, reconciliation, adoption into the family, sonship with the most high God, and an inheritance with the saints forever. "For to me to live is Christ," summarized his outlook (Philippians 1:21a). Paul owed an incalculable debt. But when he approached Christ on bended knee with overflowing heart to try to repay this debt, he ever found the Savior with outstretched hand and pointed finger, saying, "Go ye into all the world." This incalculable, inestimable debt was transferred by Christ toward those who needed Paul's ministry. He owed to them all that he owed to Christ. They held the promissory note.

The indebtedness that grows from repentance pertains to every believer. It attaches to all who receive forgiveness. Each Christian comes to the Lord and says, "I know you don't need anything, let alone anything I have to give. But, God, what I do have is yours, and I will regard the debt I owe to you as owed to whomever you wish me to serve in your name." Everyone who has received the gospel has received it as a steward, responsible to the God who gave it and to all others for whom it is intended. The obligation is universal in the church. It descends upon each of us.

Thanks for nothing

I talked to a man who said he had given up the church and Christianity because it seemed to him that the idea was that he was supposed to be under some debt of gratitude to God. He did not like that idea. He did not feel grateful at all, so he quit going to church. It soon was obvious why he felt that way. Unlike Paul, he had not received salvation; he had not received an inheritance with the saints; he had not become a new creature in Jesus Christ; he had not been given all things. So far as he knew, he had received nothing at all. He was precisely that grateful.

One cannot share what is not possessed. For many the attitude of Paul is absolutely alien. They cannot understand him at all. For Paul it was equally unthinkable that he had been given much and would do nothing in return. "I am obligated," he said to the world.

And with that he set forth to cut a swath across the continent with the glorious gospel of Christ. And the cause of Christ has advanced around the globe to the extent that repentant people felt that way:

"I am debtor," cried William Carey as he sailed for India with the gospel.

"I am debtor," cried David Livingstone as he plunged into the interior of Africa, going where Europeans had never before been seen.

"I am debtor," cried Hudson Taylor as he approached the hundreds of millions in China.

"I am debtor," cried Lord Shaftsbury as he gave himself to the poor, helpless, homeless, ragged urchins of the slums of London.

"I am debtor," cried Florence Nightingale as she followed the trail of battlefield blood to bind the wounded and care for the dying.

"I am debtor," cried Kagawa as he took the gospel to the slums of Tokyo.

We are morally bound to pay the debts of forgiveness. Unfortunately, what most of us must now repent of is how little we have regarded what God has done for us. If you do not feel that he has, that is your problem.

Your first love

If you do know Christ you may be like many who began their walk of faith aflame with love for God. But somewhere along the line the flame has dwindled from lack of fuel. You have not continued to put on the belt of truth of Ephesians 6, digging out those dark corners and filling their emptiness with affection for God.

Jesus came by way of letter to the great city of Ephesus, which was renowned for its idolatry, in particular its licentious worship of the goddess Diana. Ruins have been uncovered from vast brothels that flourished in the city. But Jesus did not condemn those things with laser-like words. He took aim instead at the Christian community and said, "I have somewhat against thee, because thou hast left thy first love. Remember therefore from whence thou art fallen, and repent, and do the first works; or else I will come unto thee quickly, and will remove thy candlestick out of his place, except thou repent" (Revelation 2:4–5).

Surely these words cut to the hearts of the Ephesian Christians. This was meant to be radical surgery. Today he comes to us with eyes of flame to illumine the deep, dark corners we have failed to sweep out ourselves. He pronounces his judgment: "You have left your first love!"

For all the blessings we have received, few feel Paul's obligation; most have never lifted a finger to labor for Christ. Some think coming to church, sitting in a pew and listening half-attentively to a sermon is labor. The lips strain to mumble a prayer. The mind struggles to pay attention rather than think of the ball game that will be on television in the afternoon. This is the life that needs to be transformed through the religious affections that grow out of awakened feelings of obligation to God. The life of the Christian needs to be rebroken and reshaped.

There was much for the Ephesians to rejoice in. They had labored tirelessly and borne persecution in the midst of an ungodly city. They had had no truck with wickedness. They had rebuked those who taught impure doctrine. Were we members of that church we probably would be feeling smug about our high level of spirituality. Yet Christ does not rebuke the village atheists, the debauched revelers, and the frauds outside the community of faith. The Ephesians' problem lay in a lack of heart affection, the fruit of thankful, contrite repentance. No matter how a married couple works to keep the house tidy, the dishes washed, and the beds made, if their hearts lack love for one another that marriage is in trouble. In Revelation 2 Jesus Christ the bridegroom draws the bride to the side and says, "What has happened to your love for me? There is something amiss with our relationship because your ardor for me has cooled."

Take a moment to put on the belt of truth right now and evaluate your heart response of affection. If you are a Christian there was a day—you remember it well—when God lifted the veil from your mind and the scales from your eyes and you looked upon the cross. The twins of faith and repentance overwhelmed you as, for the first time, you understood for whom the Savior died. How your heart melted by the fire of that redeeming love. You embraced Christ with tears of gratitude. You were made new, and all things around you seemed new. Your heart nearly burst with song, and you delighted to go to him in prayer. It was pure joy to meditate on new truths in Scripture. Times spent with God's people in worship were sacred. It was so disappointing that there were no more times your small group could meet for prayer and fellowship. Why did so few seem to come back for Sunday night worship when the praise songs and sharing times were so edifying? You loved Christ with a love like that of Samuel Rutherford. One of the authors of the *Westminster Confession*, this Puritan's love for Christ was intense. Rutherford said that, though a river drawn from hell separated Christ from him, he gladly would have plunged in and waded across, so that he might be with his Beloved. This is a first love.

But something happened to your first love. It became harder to get up on Sunday morning. The preacher was invariably boring and talked far too long. The day that was holy became a day of chores or personal or family fun. You can't wait to get out to desecrate the Sabbath, to give it over to things of the world. The glitter and allure of worldliness once seemed to be of little interest as you basked in Christ's sun. Now it seems strangely bright again, and you cannot seem to see heaven as clearly. The pleasures of the body have become more important than the prosperity of the soul.

Remember the height

There is a two-part remedy for the sickness of having left your first love: (1) remember and (2) repent. Repentance again holds the key to renewal. Scripture often calls us to remember the eager times gone by. For the Ephesians it wasn't that long. This was the A.D. 90s, and many older members of the church could remember the glory years when Paul taught daily and the people grew in numbers and spiritual life.

Do you remember the joyous discovery that life could be different than it had been, that hatred and bitterness and strife did not have to rule, that the past did not have to enslave? Remember that freedom?

Do you remember the intimate quiet times alone with him, perhaps by the beach or under a sharply scented pine tree? Remember the serendipity of being shown a new idea by the Holy Spirit?

Do you remember . . . ?

If we find ourselves far from God, he has not moved. Remember the height from which we have fallen? Notice that Jesus does not tell the Ephesians that they have slipped or declined in their love but that they have fallen. It is a drastic, serious thing. But we are not far from where we were in the proximity of repentance. Charles Spurgeon said:

Men come to Christ for the first time, of a sudden, in a moment. We receive it in an instant, like a gift from a king, the gift of eternal life. We are born anew in a moment as a child is born into this world. It is of a sudden that we repent and are converted the first time. And so it is, as I have noted throughout all the years of my ministry, that when people return unto God, they come back with a leap, in a moment; of a sudden they repent and return to him.

You can no more return to Christ slowly than you could come to Christ slowly. You just remember, repent, and return, doing what you did in the beginning.

As a faithful Physician, Christ not only prescribes the remedy but observes the consequences for failing to take it. For a church this was serious—"I will come to you and remove your lampstand from its place." You will cease to be a functioning part of the body of Christ, disqualified as a true church. A great many religious organizations get together to "play church" but have no reality. They are just going through the motions and will likely never repent because they have few or no saved members. They are a ghost ship cast adrift.

In freezing temperatures a person suffering from exposure and hypothermia may suffer at first, but then the pain lessens and a certain feeling of warmth spreads through the body. It would be fine to simply sit in the snow and go to sleep. There will be time to get inside later. Only later never comes. It is so with the church. We will either repent and do the first works or we will rebel against the Spirit of God and find ourselves slipping deeper into a fatal slumber from which we shall never rise. Individuals cannot lose their salvation if in Christ. Churches have no such assurance, and I fear that a great many have already slid into oblivion without missing a single Sunday service.

Brokenness before God—the buckling on of the belt of truth—means ultimate victory. Weakness in God's army assures strength: "To him who overcomes, I will give the right to eat from the tree of life, which is in the paradise of God." We started in a garden, and life is pointed toward another garden, one in which our first place of fellowship with God will be re-created. Meanwhile we are in the spiritual battlefield, where we need absolute dependence on God—the dependence that only repentance grows.

What assurances does the Christian have in death?

Death, being the wages of sin, why are not the righteous delivered from death, seeing all their sins are forgiven in Christ? The righteous shall be delivered from death itself at the last day, and even in death are delivered from the sting and curse of it; so that, although they die, yet it is out of God's love, to free them perfectly from sin and misery, and to make them capable of further communion with Christ, in glory, which they then enter upon. [Westminster Larger Catechism, question 85]

The Stinger Is Gone

Evangelism Explosion witnessing teams have asked millions of people a question that I now ask: Have you come to a place in your spiritual life where you know for certain that if you were to die today you would go to heaven?

You may think you don't have to face that issue today, but you really don't know whether you will see another sunset. Unless Christ returns soon, there will be a day on which you will die. At this point, earthly life is not open-ended. Your situation is terminal, and you will either face that final day of change with confidence or with dread and fear.

This book is about transformed living through Jesus Christ, who makes all things new. No one lives a transformed life until he or she settles the matter of death. I believe one reason for the fear that so infests our churches arises from a weakness in faithfulness to the Word of God regarding the future hope of the believer.

I see three reasons for fearing death:

1. You have no adequate answer to the question of where you will spend eternity. You are in rebel-

lion against God, and you have no ground for hope that he will accept you.

2. You have accepted Christ as Lord and Savior but believe that, at any moment, you may sin and fall from grace. Perhaps you have been taught that even one unconfessed sin will send you to hell or to some netherworld of purgatory. Perhaps you believe that you will be prepared for eternity only through doing the right things in the right way and having the right prayers said over your dying form.

> *I am the resurrection, and the life: he that believeth in me, though he were dead, yet shall he live: And whosoever liveth and believeth in me shall never die. Believest thou this?* [John 11:25–26]

3. Something clouds your eyes. Maybe it is worldliness, for you have neglected your love of the Lord. At the very least you would feel uncomfortable standing in God's presence when you have sought to be with him so rarely. Or perhaps you feel depressed and confused as you now approach death through age or illness. You should be happy about going to be with the Lord, but pain, fear of the process of dying, and the prospect of being cut off from those you love have stolen away any joy.

If you are in any of those categories, life is just waiting to be transformed. Death is an enemy with a poisonous sting, but the stinger has been pulled for the Christian. You can know how to answer the question of where you will spend eternity. You can be transformed by that knowledge.

Living with dying

To put into perspective our fears and hopes regarding death, we need to be certain we understand that three periods of life are involved. First, there is a time of preparing to die and of dealing with death. How a person lives tells a lot about how prepared he or she is to die. But feelings grow more intense when someone we love, whose fellowship and presence are important, is taken. Feelings intensify when a physician gives us the news that some illness or physical condition has erupted to herald the end of earthly life. That news is a shock for which few are immediately ready. Feelings intensify when we begin to experience the draining of vitality or mental coherency and bouts of searing, unbearable pain.

Second, there is the moment of death itself. It is a dramatic point of passage, about which those who have undergone clinical death and been revived can perhaps tell us a little. The closest analogy that the dying human has personally experienced previous to this moment is birth. Not many remember that day in their lives, and few infants seem thrilled to be going through it. One anticipating heaven may be forgiven a little queasiness about that instant when the body shuts down and an unknown reality opens.

Third, there is the new reality itself, what theologians refer to as the "intermediate state" between death and the resurrection and the "final state" after the resurrection and last judgment.

The Bible shares some very human reactions to death, and a surprising divine reaction. Jesus, who in John 11 said, "I am the resurrection, and the life" moments later watched the sorrow of the grieving friends and family of Lazarus and the look of the enclosed tomb—and cried. Jesus was about to raise Lazarus's body from the grave. He knew that this episode would have a joyous ending for these standing around the final resting place. Yet he still cried. Jesus' tears say something significant: Death doesn't just hurt us. It also hurts God. Death and hell were never intended to be our best. They have become our best through the cross of Jesus, but they still hurt God because they are the grievous fruit of human corruption in sin.

Death, then, is not in itself a joyful occasion. The Old Testament in particular records a human perspective of death as separation and ending. This sorrow is not condemned by Scripture. Rather these bittersweet passages reflect that people were made to give glory to and enjoy God forever within bodies. Sin has affected this ideal in life and in death:

> There the wicked cease from troubling; and there the weary be at rest. There the prisoners rest together; they hear not the voice of the oppressor. The small and great are there; and the servant is free from his master. . . . One dieth in his full strength, being wholly at ease and quiet. His breasts are full of milk, and his bones are moistened with marrow. And another dieth in the bitterness of his soul, and never eateth with pleasure. They shall lie down alike in the dust, and the worms shall cover them. [Job 3:17–19; 21:23–26]

> Be not thou afraid when one is made rich, when the glory of his house is increased; For when he dieth he

shall carry nothing away: his glory shall not descend after him. [Psalm 49:16–17]

There is no man that hath power over the spirit to retain the spirit; neither hath he power in the day of death. [Ecclesiastes 8:8a]

For the grave cannot praise thee, death can not celebrate thee: they that go down into the pit cannot hope for thy truth. [Isaiah 38:18]

But one morning the sting was taken out of death. On that morning the grave became a less fearful place. A little boy with a serious allergy to bee venom was riding in the car with his father. It was a warm day and the windows were rolled down. Suddenly the two of them heard an angry buzz from the back seat. The air currents had pulled a bumblebee into the car, and he was angry, just looking for someone to sting. Knowing that a bee sting could bring on a fatal allergic reaction, the boy started screaming as the bee came over the seat, closer and closer. Then suddenly the bee just disappeared.

"It's all right, son," said the father. "That bee can't sting you now." It was true, for the father had reached out and caught the bee in his hand and thrown him out the window. All that was left was the stinger in the father's palm. Paul said:

O death, where is thy sting? O grave, where is thy victory? The sting of death is sin; and the strength of sin is the law. But thanks be to God, which giveth us the victory through our Lord Jesus Christ. [1 Corinthians 15:55–57]

As a result the New Testament looks not at the lonely grave but at the victorious sunrise. Death continues what the Christian has in life—the opportunity to glorify God and to enjoy him forever:

> But ye are come unto mount Sion, and unto the city of the living God, the heavenly Jerusalem, and to an innumerable company of angels, To the general assembly and church of the firstborn, which are written in heaven, and to God the Judge of all, and to the spirits of just men made perfect, And to Jesus the mediator of the new covenant, and to the blood of sprinkling, that speaketh better things than that of Abel. [Hebrews 12:22–24]

Death is a time of freedom from the bonds of sin:

> For we know that if our earthly house of this tabernacle were dissolved, we have a building of God, an house not made with hands, eternal in the heavens. For in this we groan, earnestly desiring to be clothed upon with our house which is from heaven: If so be that being clothed we shall not be found naked. For we that are in this tabernacle do groan, being burdened: not for that we would be unclothed, but clothed upon, that mortality might be swallowed up of life. Now he that hath wrought us for the selfsame thing is God, who also hath given unto us the earnest of the Spirit. [2 Corinthians 5:1–5]

Death is a time of intimacy with our Lord:

> And he [the thief hanging next to Jesus on the cross] said unto Jesus, Lord, remember me when thou comest into thy kingdom. And Jesus said unto him, Verily I say unto thee, Today shalt thou be with me in paradise. [Luke 23:42–43]

> Therefore we are always confident, knowing that, whilst we are at home in the body, we are absent from the Lord: (For we walk by faith, not by sight:) We are confident,

I say, and willing rather to be absent from the body, and to be present with the Lord. [2 Corinthians 5:6–8]

For to me to live is Christ, and to die is gain. But if I live in the flesh, this is the fruit of my labour: yet what I shall choose I wot not. For I am in a strait betwixt two, having a desire to depart, and to be with Christ; which is far better: Nevertheless to abide in the flesh is more needful for you. [Philippians 1:21–24]

Death is a time of peace:

And I heard a voice from heaven saying unto me, Write, Blessed are the dead which die in the Lord from henceforth: Yea, saith the Spirit, that they may rest from their labours; and their works do follow them. [Revelation 14:13]

Getting ready for the last day of life

It is no longer necessary to fear death. Yet, given the sinfulness of human beings and the holiness of God, one who has not repented of sin and rested in Jesus Christ for salvation has every right to be afraid to die. It would be irrational not to be afraid to stand before the God of the Bible without a covering of righteousness.

The way modern men and women have chosen to deal with that fear is through denial. Take for example these new trends in mortuary science:

The body is no longer a corpse. It is "the departed," "the loved one," or "Mr. Smith. "

Mr. Smith is no longer "laid out" for viewing. He is in the "slumber room."

Lipstick and rouge have been making departed ones look "so natural, just like he's sleeping" for a long time. But at some funeral parlors Mr. Smith may be stretched out on a couch with a book or his favorite pipe, waiting to greet visitors.

Death, like religion and politics, is not polite conversation. Was it ever? Well, yes. One group of Christians who spoke about death quite a lot were the Puritans. That may seem to go along with history's portrait of them as morbid killjoys. The Puritans actually were among the most joyous and fun-loving of peoples. They were nothing like the romanticized portrayal on Thanksgiving cards or the superpious fuddy-duddy image that goes with the epithet *puritanical*. But the journals, letters, books, and sermons they left mention death far more often than would make modern Americans comfortable. One reason the Puritans in the American colonies had much to say about death was that frontier life was hard and often brief. But also, Puritan writers speak of contemplating their own death each day to keep things in perspective, to grow in wisdom and self-understanding. Thinking of their death was a reality check on evaluating the important things. It helped the Puritans fasten their thoughts securely on the "sweetness of the Savior." That gave life and death full meaning. They put to practical action the words of Psalm 90:12: "So teach us to number our days, that we may apply our hearts unto wisdom."

If you want to judge what gives life meaning, I direct your attention to a number of testimonies—the last words of those who had contemplated the sweetness of the Savior and those who had not. Some had answered that question of where they would go if they died today, and some had not given it a thought.

W. C. Fields was quite ill in the hospital, and a friend was astonished upon entering the hospital room to find this irreligious man thumbing through the pages of a

Bible. The friend remarked, "Is that really you, reading the Bible?"

Fields replied, "I'm just looking for a loophole."

Even for Fields, such flippancy rings hollow as he wandered from a godless life toward a godless eternity. The loophole he sought was there in those pages he was holding: He could become a man made new through the blood of Jesus Christ. One man who found that loophole was Hermann Lange, a young German preacher who stood among the Christians who spoke out against Adolf Hitler's repression of the gospel. Like many others Lange was arrested, interrogated, tried as a criminal, and condemned to die before a firing squad. On the last day of his life he wrote a farewell letter to his parents:

> When this letter comes to your hands, I shall no longer be among the living. The thing that has occupied our thoughts constantly for many months, never leaving them free, is now about to happen. If you ask me what state I am in, I can only answer: I am, first, in a joyous mood, and second, filled with great anticipation. As regards the first feeling, today means the end of all suffering and all earthly sorrow for me—and "God will wipe away every tear" from my eyes. What consolation, what marvelous strength emanates from faith in Christ, who has preceded us in death. In him, I have put my faith, and precisely today I have faith in him more firmly than ever. . . . Look where you will [in Scripture] . . . rejoice, once more I say to you, rejoice. And as to the second feeling [of anticipation] this day brings the greatest hour of my life! Everything that till now I have done, struggled for, and accomplished has at bottom been directed to this one goal, whose barrier I shall penetrate today. "Eye hath not seen, nor ear heard, neither have entered into the heart of man, the things which God hath prepared for them that love him"

(1 Corinthians 2:9). . . . Should I not then be filled with
anticipation? What is it all going to be like? . . . I return
to the home of my Father. . . . Until we meet again above
in the presence of the Father of Light,

Your joyful Hermann.

Juxtapose the last words of unbelievers and the last
words of believers, and it can hardly be imagined that
they are speaking of the same event. Lange approached
death with such anticipation and joy. Was it feigned?
The result of psychological stress from imprisonment?
Or had he come to grips with the question of his eternal destiny and as a result faced death with confidence?
Contrast the following deathbed statements:

"I am going into eternity, and it is sweet for me to
think of eternity," said David Brainerd, missionary.

"I am abandoned by God and man! I shall go to
Hell!" cried Voltaire.

"Doctor, I am dying, but I am not afraid to die. 'Tis
well," said George Washington.

"It is hell to be left alone," said Thomas Paine.

"I die in the faith of Jesus Christ, and in the firm
hope of a better life," said Michelangelo.

"How were the circus receipts today at Madison
Square Garden?" asked P. T. Barnum, who had judged
himself in his famous line: "There's a sucker born every
minute."

"Earth is receding, and heaven is opening, and this
is my coronation day," said evangelist Dwight L.
Moody.

Many such last lines have breathed remorse, horror,
fear, grief, pained acceptance, hope, contentment, and
joy. Few approach the end of life without two strong
emotions, one that looks back on what has been and
one that looks forward on what will come next. Except
for a Barnum who is counting his receipts to the last,

death has a way of changing one's perspective. In my collection of dying words I even have one from the militant atheist Robert Ingersoll, who spent his adult life trying to convince the world that God did not exist. "If there be a God, may he have mercy on my soul," cried this suddenly uncertain atheist.

If you have not come to the point where you know for certain that you are called, justified, adopted, and sanctified, I direct your attention to the day of your death. It may come when you least expect, and when you are unprepared to take up unfinished business with the Creator of heaven and earth. But it need not be like that. Death left its stinger in Jesus. It can no longer destroy those who have taken refuge under his scarred hands.

Held safely

There are Christians who yet live in the oppressive fear that they may face God without Christ. We have already said that it is not possible to fall from God's grace before the end (see p. 103). Can a person who has been regenerated ever become unregenerated? Can a person who has received eternal life at the hand of an unchanging God go to hell forever or to a place somewhere between heaven and hell as the Roman Catholic Church has described purgatory? There is neither truth nor victory in such theology. It needlessly steals away the transforming hope that is by right the Christian's.

Let us look at the various answers to this question.

The Roman Catholic Church historically says that yes, a person can fall away. One can no longer speak of a monolithic Catholic theology, for the church of Rome stands divided over many of its historical doctrines. A modernism that looks only to this life for the coming of the kingdom of God and regards hope in heaven to be a distraction from the fight for social justice has pulled the church from one side. A new openness to study the Scriptures has pulled many Catholics in the evangelical direction. A charismatic renewal movement pulls in yet a third way. Historically and still dominant in Roman theology, however, is a belief that salvation belongs not to the individual Christian but to the institutional church as a community of believers. The church is the tap that dispenses God's grace. Individual faith pleases God only if accompanied by righteous living in connection with the sacraments and love. At the very least, the Roman Church teaches, a time of purging will prepare one for heaven. But no consistent Roman Catholic is ever even certain to qualify for purgatory. No consistent Catholic says, "I know I am eternally in the hand of God."

Lutheran doctrine likewise makes perseverance uncertain, teaching that a truly converted Christian can come to lose or reject faith, and as a result lose grace as well, forfeiting justification by treason. No consistent Lutheran says, "I know I am eternally in the hand of God."

Neither does that group of churches whose theology is known as *Arminianism* teach that Christians are safe. Since their view of salvation is born of a high view of the individual will, many say emphatically that a person may be saved and then lost. Many ride a roller coaster of emotion, now high and secure, now backslidden and unsure. A person may be saved and lost literally hundreds of times, and at the grieving, loved ones must wonder, "In which state was his or her soul at the moment of death?" That will determine whether the person is in heaven or hell.

Calvinists can consistently say that no person who has been truly saved can ever be lost. I have listed biblical reasons for their statement (see pp. 103–106).

Romans 11:29 (NIV) summarizes the trust that "God's gifts and his call are irrevocable." Salvation is as certain as the promise of God. Security has limits. Jesus warns in Matthew 10:22; 24:13 and Mark 13:13: "But he that shall endure unto the end, the same shall be saved." It doesn't mean that any confessor of Jesus lives for the world, the flesh, and the devil and then goes to heaven. There is no question about the fact that those who do not persevere to the end will not be saved. But the one who has turned away from sin to live for God need never fear disqualification from sin or failure. Christ intends that those who come to him share the confidence of the Christian who was asked, "Are you not afraid that you will slip through his fingers!"

That Christian replied, "I *am* one of his fingers."

The rescuer

Then there are those in that third category, Christians whose knees knock and whose feet shake. They are like the preacher who had just seen the Holy Spirit work in a revival service until he felt giddy with rejoicing in God's love and mercy as he returned to his hotel room for the night. He hardly noticed the storm clouds boiling overhead, and when he dropped to his knees he prayed, "Oh, that right now might be the moment of your final return!"

Just then a bolt of lightning split the sky just outside his window, and the accompanying thunder crack just about sent him through the ceiling. "Wait! Not *quite* yet!" he shouted above the din.

My own emotions remain quite mixed as I contemplate the Lord I serve reviewing the most intimate details of my weak discipleship. I am sure I shall feel quite naked and unprepared. Yet I also know that this will be a judgment of love. Contemplating death, the Christian, like the Puritans, should use that expectation to judge life now, so as not to fear words of rebuke later. "I must work the works of him that sent me, while it is day," said Jesus, "the night cometh when no man can work" (John 9:4).

The mind contemplating death can certainly think of much unfinished business. What can a pastor say to a dying young cancer victim with a toddler at her knee who will not be there to care for the hurts or know the joys of seeing this young one reach adulthood? When a child dies or a newlywed buries her young husband, doubts cloud the mind. Where is God's love and plan in this? And I must say, "It is there, just beyond sight." For I don't know the plan, but I know the Planner. He wept at the grave of Lazarus, feeling the suffering that sin's legacy on humanity was causing. He hurts when his children hurt, and he will work it all for good in a way we may least expect.

The mind contemplating death may also be distracted by a fear that the final struggle with pain or the loss of mental function that comes with some diseases may be more than bearable. A time may come when pain or sorrow steals away the feeling of victory. The believer may slip and fall flat as upon the deck of a rolling ship. That is when the *Westminster Confession's* promise of perseverance becomes so precious. A dramatic film was made on the life of Jan Hus, the Bohemian preacher who read the works of John Wycliffe and was transformed in his faith. In 1414 he was called to defend his teachings at the Council of Constance. Though promised safe conduct to present his case, he was arrested upon his arrival at the council, summarily tried for heresy, and sentenced to burn. One scene of the film shows the reformer writing by the light of a candle in his cell. He puts down his quill and studies the flame, then puts his hand above it. The pain makes him draw back quickly. Will he be able to stand when he can no longer draw away from the heat?

I don't know whether the real Hus went through the moment of doubt this film portrayed. I do know that as he was chained to the stake Hus looked upward to heaven and said, "Father, into thy hands I commit my spirit."

When Jesus said those same words on the cross he had become sin for all of us, and had experienced the most terrible experience the Son of God could possibly know, the wrath of a just God punishing sin. The Father turned his back on the Son, yet at the moment of death the Son knew that the Father was the One into whose hands he could commit his spirit. For he had already breathed the shout of victory: "It is finished!" Sin's atonement was accomplished. The stinger of death was still releasing its venom, but it was pulled from the bee, never again to strike out at the people of God. So when Hus reached his moment of crisis, he knew there was One on whom he could cast himself, with all his natural human feelings of pain and terror.

Deliverance assured

The question from the *Westminster Larger Catechism* heading this chapter addresses a natural human response: If our sins have been taken away, why do we still have to go through death at all? Why not just be translated from one shore to the other, as an Enoch or an Elijah? The answer gives two responses. First, a day is coming when that will indeed happen. Second, meanwhile, the death of a Christian has been transformed from something dreadful to a beautiful response of God's love. It has become a door to freedom from the state of sin and misery that still plagues the world. It has become a door open to communion with Christ in glory, which the Christian may freely enter and partake. "Precious in the sight of the LORD is the death of his saints" (Psalm 116:15).

If you fear the accompanying pain and affliction of the last enemy or the moment of passage into something unknown, you have a God on which you can cast that burden—a God who has blazed the trail before you. He has defeated the enemy and removed the stinger.

If you fear death because you have no answer for the question of where you would spend eternity if you died today, then you do not have the transforming salvation this book has explained. You may have gone to some altar rail forty years ago. You may be a deacon, an elder, a minister, a teacher, but if your heart holds the dread of uncertainty, you need to give your life to the Christ who has taken the fear out of death for the child of God.

Why does the Christian not fear death? Most simply, it is because the Christian will never die. Someday, when my friends and family gather around for the obsequies, I want you to know that I will be more alive then than I am at this moment. Our bodies may be laid out, but we shall be very much alive, and the bonds will be broken forever.

Study Guide

Introduction

Words to define

newness	gospel	grace
heaven	gift	faith

Points to ponder

1. People can change in many ways through particular experiences and the stages of life. But only Christ makes all things new.

2. The themes of Scripture we will approach are transforming themes of salvation.

3. Five words that transform lives: grace, man, God, Christ, faith.

Questions to answer

1. Suppose a psychologist were studying the lives of war prisoner Jacob DeShazar and disillusioned war hero

Mitsuo Fuchida before they became Christians. What changes in their lives might the psychologist prescribe? If we add in their spiritual needs, how does this analysis change?

2. Would anyone looking at these men have predicted the ways in which they did, in fact, change? Draw some distinctions between the world's idea of rehabilitation and the kingdom of God's idea of becoming new.

3. Imagine that you are a Job who has lost all possessions, family, and health. What might you look to for hope or comfort? To be of benefit, what must that source give?

4. Was the life of the drunken father whose addiction had cost his daughter's life worth changing? Perhaps you know of someone whose life has become new in Christ, and those around wonder why God would waste salvation on such a person. Is there an answer to such a question?

5. Why might this drunken father have rejected the gospel message?

6. Why does the chapter say that many people, and our society itself, are dying of spiritual malnourishment?

Notebook

If you have not done so, begin a notebook to collect thoughts and impressions about the plan of salvation this book will cover. Start by copying the five words *grace, man, God, Christ,* and *faith.* Describe how each of those words represents something God has done in your life. Perhaps you can share the resulting testimony with someone. If you aren't sure what those words mean to you, ask God to show you through his Word.

Chapter 1: All Things Are Made New

Words to define

quest questions
born again
metamorphosis
mediator

Messiah
prophet
priest
savior

catholic church
king
judge

Points to ponder

1. The only kind of Christian is the one who has been born again.

2. The *Westminster Confession* speaks of a series of steps in the plan of salvation: *redemption, calling, justification, sanctification,* and *glorification.*

3. Jesus is the anointed Prophet, Priest, and King. Jesus is God; this means God chose himself to fulfil the total need of lost humanity.

Questions to answer

1. Why is *rebirth* an accurate word to describe what happens when a person enters the kingdom of God? Read John 3. What is the work of the Father in this rebirth? The Son? The Holy Spirit?

2. Why did the mediator of the new covenant have to be God? Why did he have to be human?

3. If Jesus came to earth to die for lost men and women, why did he have to go through the stages of growing up with parents and brothers and sisters? Why did he preach, teach, heal, and cast out demons?

4. Since the Old Testament provided quite a lot of information about the Messiah who was coming, why did the Jewish leaders not recognize Jesus? Why should Gentiles care that Jesus was the Jewish Messiah?

5. If Jesus is a king, what is the Christian's relationship to governments of this world? What kind of nation does Jesus rule? Why isn't it a more unified nation?

6. Who is included in the catholic church?

7. What must the lost sinner do to partake of the promise in John 3:16 of everlasting life?

Notebook

Is Jesus still a prophet, a priest, and a king today? Think through each of the offices that Jesus fulfils in your life. How does he reveal God to you? Read Hebrews 9. Beyond his offering of himself as a sacrifice for your sin, do you benefit in other ways from his priesthood? Is he the king in your life? If so, how do you acknowledge his rule?

Chapter 2: The Hound of Heaven

Words to define

internal call   predestination   ordained
external call   irresistible grace   Arminian
effectual call   elect   Calvinist

Points to ponder

1. The grace of God is available and calls out to every person on earth, but none come without an inward call to the heart by the Holy Spirit.

2. God's working in the individual's heart draws that person from one worldview to another, so that life begins to be brought into conformity with the will of God.

3. The bottom line of salvation is that there is nothing in a Christian that makes him or her more worthy

of God's mercy than the non-Christian. The only difference is God's will—not the person's.

Questions to answer

1. What did Francis Thompson convey to us when
he put the words in the mouth of the hound of heaven:
"All things betray thee, who betrayest me"?

2. What is the work of the Holy Spirit in the call of
God? What is the work of Christians in that call?

3. Does predestination mean that a person has no part
in his or her salvation? Why does Scripture teach that
only those God has given to Jesus will come to him?

4. If it is the Holy Spirit who works grace in the
heart, why should we pray for the salvation of anyone?
Why should we send missionaries or invite people to
turn and believe?

5. Does grace keep drawing us on in faith and obedience once we have accepted Christ as our Savior?
Why is it that some Christians seem to remain forever
in spiritual diapers, without maturing in their lives?

6. What are the dangers or temptations for the Christian who does not believe there to be an effectual call
of God? Are there also dangers and temptations for
Christians who do believe there to be that call?

7. What is the great blessing that belongs to one who
accepts his or her call to be God's ambassador?

Notebook

You may wish to find the complete poem, "The Hound
of Heaven," and read this dramatic vision of God's
pursuing love. Think back over your own life and write
down ways that God's grace pursued you before you
knew him. Did you once put confidence in the flesh as
Paul did? (See Phil. 3:4b–6.)

Chapter 3: Forgiveness to the Uttermost

Words to define

justification   objective guilt   anxiety
pardon   ultimate guilt   legalism
imputation   guilt feelings   conscience

Points to ponder

1. Only a holy and omnipotent God can declare someone just.

2. Only because a worthy substitute has been found can we be declared righteous by God.

3. Justification is the final answer for guilt and the separation that exists between a person and God. There is access to God and no longer the need to fear hell.

Questions to answer

1. Why is our justification before God the "foremost pillar of religion"?

2. What is the difference between a judge declaring a person "not guilty" and declaring the person "not liable for punishment"? How can God declare us guilty yet not liable for punishment, pardoned and positively righteous through Jesus Christ?

3. Why does a person who has been justified still feel a badness and a need for self-punishment?

4. What can true, objective guilt do for the unbeliever? For the believer?

5. How did Jesus pull Peter back from guilt by making him thrice affirm love and allegiance?

6. What can be transformed in the believer's life by the knowledge of justification? What does the justified person have before God?

7. Why does the person who is justified still have problems with sin?

Notebook

From a human standpoint the vital fact about our justification is that we can provide nothing to the process except faith. We are found guilty but justified in the sight of a holy God only because Christ stood in our place, accepting our punishment so that we might stand in Christ's place, taking his righteousness. Write down some ways that faith—trusting in Christ alone—should change a person's attitude toward acts of obedience to God and acts of disobedience to him. Are our acts of obedience truly good?

Chapter 4: Abba, Daddy

Words to define

adoption   universalism   citizenship
sonship   brotherhood   heir
ordo salutis

Points to ponder

1. Because of justification we can stand before God; because of adoption we can have intimacy with God, returning us to the kind of closeness that Adam and Eve enjoyed before the fall.

2. Adam was created to be in the relationships of son and citizen. The one who trusts Jesus as Savior and

Lord is re-created to be in those relationships and cannot break them as did Adam.

3. *Abba* fatherhood allows the child of God a place in the kingdom, with a new name, a new spirit, access to God through prayer, intimacy, an inheritance, and an eternal home.

Questions to answer

1. How do election and justification relate to our adoption by God? Why might we call adoption the ultimate blessing of the Christian life?

2. How does the Christian's adoption affect his or her relationship with God? With Jesus? With other Christians?

3. What is wrong with the idea that we are brothers and sisters with everyone on earth? Does rejecting the idea of the universal fatherhood of God and the brotherhood of humanity mean that we do not care about the lives and souls of the lost? What must we reject in this univeralist concept of the Father?

4. What does it mean to be a true child of Abraham? God set apart the physical descendants of Abraham as the nation of Israel. How did God set apart the spiritual descendants of Abraham?

5. Neither punishment nor chastisement is pleasant. From Hebrews 12:4–13, how does one know whether a hardship is God's discipline of a child and not a judge's punishment of a felon? What does this passage say about the purpose of God's fatherly chastisement?

6. How is the Holy Spirit like the genetic connection between a child and his parents? How does God offer a new name in his family connection with a child?

7. What does the fatherhood of God mean to one who feels overwhelmed by the storms of life?

Notebook

In John 8:31–59 Jesus uses harsh language to describe those who thought they were automatically children of God because of the right ancestry. Do you know someone who thinks a godly parent or grandparent is a ticket to heaven? What would you share with them about the true fatherhood of the heavenly Father?

Chapter 5: The Glint of Gold

Words to define

perfection   perseverance   conformity to the
connectedness   identification   pattern
sanctification

Points to ponder

1. Sanctification is the life-long process of bringing the life of the child of God into conformity with Christ, a work of renewing and enabling that transforms all that a person is, thinks, and does.

2. The person who is being sanctified knows intellectually who Jesus is and what he has done, emotionally accepts Christ's sacrifice, and then submits to the rule of Christ in life.

Questions to answer

1. What did the Holy Spirit do in the preacher, the woman, and her father-in-law to bring the man to repent? Did the Spirit's work differ in the hearts of the Christians from that in the heart of the unbeliever?

2. Is sanctification simply a matter of living the Christian life? What is the difference between sanctification and justification?

3. In what sense does sanctification remove the corruption of the flesh from the believer? What does John 15:1–6 show us about God's work of sanctification in our lives?

4. Why do you suppose many Christians seem unconnected to Christ and unconcerned about this lack of connection?

5. What does it mean to you when you read Hebrews 12:28–29? How should awe and reverence for God be demonstrated in worship? In the life of the church as a body? In the family? On the job?

6. In the parable of the sower, what are the basic problems with the soils that do not sustain life? What would Jesus say about someone who claims to be a Christian yet does not bear fruit?

7. If we are not saved by works, are we sanctified by them? What part do they play in sanctification?

8. When Jesus prayed that God would sanctify his people by the truth, what did he mean?

Notebook

According to the Bible our salvation in Christ is secure because we have been given to Jesus Christ by the Father and are indwelt by the Holy Spirit. You can think of your salvation as a living proof of the triune nature of God. But what about those times when security slips away? Do you sometimes feel that your salvation is not secure? Think through the reasons for this given by the *Westminster Confession of Faith* and write down some steps for renewing your connection with Christ when you feel low and sinful.

Chapter 6: Three-Dimensional Faith

Words to define

saving faith submission to authority resting
recumbency reordered mind belief
accepting receiving

Points to ponder

1. Saving faith reorders the mind, emotions, and will around a central proposition that we are absolutely certain is true.

2. Three-dimensional saving faith accepts, receives, and rests on the promises of God.

3. The Christian's faith may be weak and often assailed, but through Christ it gains the final victory.

Questions to answer

1. Why must saving faith come from God?

2. What makes *faith* the ultimate action word of Christianity?

3. Does faith cause us to put rational thinking on hold so that we believe whatever is written in the Bible? What about when the Bible says things we "know" are untrue?

4. Are there specific steps by which to resolve apparent conflicts between science and Scripture? Are all such conflicts going to be satisfactorily resolved? What do we do with unresolved conflicts between two sources of truth?

5. Are there specific steps to take when someone's interpretation of a Scripture passage just doesn't seem logical or right? Why do people who may be very intel-

ligent sometimes follow a new interpretation into a false
lifestyle or kind of worship?

6. What would you say to someone who says that the
Bible's truth may be true for you, but he or she follows
another, equally true truth?

7. What does the idea of *recumbency* add to our
understanding of faith? What does the thought that
faith is like a conduit add?

Notebook

List the kinds of tests by which you judge the authority
of a person. Does authority sometimes just go with a
position or an achievement (a high academic degree
or some significant award of honor)? What makes the
individual worthy of trust and respect? What would
cause you to stake your life that what some person
says is dependable and true? What level of trust have
you placed in God and the truth of his revealed Word?
How do you show that trust in daily living?

Chapter 7: The Gift of a Broken Heart

Words to define

affections   absolute dependence   repentance
insufficiency   counterfeit repentance brokenness
legal strivings   pollution of sin   indebtedness

Points to ponder

1. Repentance does not save anyone, yet no one is
saved without it.

2. Understanding our sin makes us aware of our absolute dependence on God, breaking the heart and refocusing the heart's affections.

3. Buckling on the belt of truth of Ephesians 6 requires that we face up honestly to our continuing weakness. In that revealed weakness lies our ultimate victory.

Questions to answer

1. Did Peter give enough information to the crowd on the day of Pentecost so they could make an informed choice for Christ? What information did he give about Jesus? About salvation in Christ?

2. Is repentance simply being sorry about thoughts or actions or being frightened about consequences of those thoughts or actions? What does the repentance that comes from the Holy Spirit move the heart to do?

3. What are the transforming elements of true repentance in the seeking heart? Why do they transform the person's heart?

4. What part should the mind play in true repentance? What part should the emotions play? What makes the heart broken by an understanding of sin and of the holiness of God?

5. How different are human affections before and after coming to a knowledge of sin and then repenting? What is the focus of the non-Christian's affections? Of the Christian's?

6. Has the common Christian conception of sin and the lack of "legal strivings" affected attitudes toward worship and living holy, set-apart, indebted lives?

7. How does a renewed understanding of our brokenness from sin and of the believer's absolute dependence upon God help a Christian return to the first love of Jesus the Bridegroom and intimate fellowship with him?

Notebook

The Old Testament believer could express a broken spirit through bringing a sacrifice of the best of the flock to the Lord at the temple. The need for a sacrifice for our sin is met in the final atonement of Christ on the cross. Read Psalm 51 and Romans12:1–2. Note the kinds of sacrifices you can still bring in worship to God. How can you present a sacrifice of praise today?

Chapter 8: The Stinger Is Gone

Words to define

fear   intermediate state   grief
final state   security in Christ   resurrection

Points to ponder

1. Death is not a joyous occasion, and it was never God's intended best for us—until the cross transformed death into the best.

2. For the Christian, death is the dramatic passage to freedom, intimacy, and peace.

3. The Christian approaching death may slip into feelings of fear and depression, but Christ has been there before us and understands. He holds us firm, despite our feelings.

Questions to answer

1. Should Christians automatically long to die so that they can be with the Lord? Is sadness about death or fear of death a sign of faithlessness?

2. Why did Jesus cry at the graveside of Lazarus? What do his tears indicate about how God views death?

3. When Paul says that God has given us victory over the power of sin and death in the Lord Jesus Christ, what does he mean?

4. How does our society deny the reality of death? What can we gain by meditating on the approach of death, as did the Puritans?

5. What is so wrong or spiritually dangerous about theorizing that there might be a purgatory where we can work through unresolved sins and prepare for heaven?

6. What can a Christian do to prepare for life with the Lord after death?

7. If our sins have been taken away, why must we still endure physical death?

Notebook

A growing movement looks to assisted suicide and euthanasia as viable options for avoiding physical disintegration and pain. On the other hand, many feel compelled to use every available medical advance to wring every drop of life from a dying body. Think through some principles from Scripture that help us know how to submit to the will of God, respect life, and offer compassionate, appropriate care for someone who is suffering.